Migrants or Islamic Army: Europe on the Brink

Author: Shabbir H M Tankiwala

It is not just a requirement but necessary to have a roof over our head, a dream of each one of us to have a house of our own, we humans are the only species living on this Planet (Earth) who needs to pay taxes, we humans have developed such a system that we need to work to earn money to have food on the table, we need to pay our monthly bills.

Dispute over territories, the political, religious and ideological differences in Islamic countries. The war of ideologies in Muslim dominated west-Asia and north-African countries, sharp differences over religious and cultural issues, rivalries and distrust persist among Muslims. The social and political problems that viciously started in 2011 in several Islamic countries in W-Asia and N-Africa, many prominent Islamic countries brutally harmed, among the worst affected by sectarian violence and terrorism are countries like "Somalia, Libya, Yemen, Syria, Iraq and Afghanistan," political and economic system have totally collapsed and till year 2016 showing no signs of improvement, other major predominately Sunni-Muslim countries like Pakistan, Turkey and Egypt as well experiencing extreme rise in violence and terrorist activities, growing violence obviously harms economic growth hence reduces or rather decimate economic opportunities, situation in Islamic world between 2012 and 2016 will better be described as extremely chaotic and problematic.

Obviously when there is so much trouble in the country you live in because no one would like to live in such a chaotic situation, in such excruciating circumstances people would want to leave war-zones and move to safe harbour, after all we all care about our personal safety and security.

But here again, very often, when discussion is about Islamic problems, one question comes to mind of many, not just one question but many pressing questions, as we all know that **Islam** a great religion has been branded and promoted as the most peace loving **Religion of Peace**, than, Why so much chaos and distress in so many Islamic countries? Why are Muslim brothers and sisters from war-ravaged and poverty stricken Muslim countries fleeing and wants to desperately move to non-Muslim ruled countries to seek asylum or economic refuge? Another question arises, as to, Why Muslims are leaving Muslim countries and opting to settle in non-Islamic countries such as Australia, Canada, or in

America and Europe? Isn't it true that Muslims calls non-believers (all those who do not follow Islam) <u>Kafirs</u> (infidels). These are genuine questions to ask, but, who from Islamic community will answer? Have you ever wonder, Islam the most peace loving religion yet Muslims not safe in Muslim dominated and Muslim ruled countries.

With lot of hopes and dreams, between 2012 and 2015 millions of Muslim migrants and refugees have crossed into Europe, but, what better future and economic opportunities Europe can provide now or in future? As of 2015, as it is things are not rosy in European Union countries, slow economic growth, high rate of unemployment and underemployment, plus environment and climatic problems.

Islam itself a divided house, Islam divided into two faction or sect "**Shiite and Sunni**," both faction consider each other illegitimate, so Islam is divided along sectarian and cultural lines, brutal Islamic problems, wars and civil wars, sectarian strife in many Islamic countries, Islamic problems have created problems for Europeans and also not spared the Americans, sadly the internal Islamic issues and difficulties have divided and cause sharp division within western countries as well.

While the optimists who allegedly have soft corner for Islam in Europe wants to welcome refugees, and they argue that refugees will in long term help Europe, valuable contribution from large immigrant population will help spur European economic growth.

But another large section of European population do not agree with the optimists, and fiercely oppose any move of providing asylum to migrants and refugees who apparently are coming inside Europe from predominately Muslim countries and majority are followers of Sunni Islam, and they are of the opinion and says "**They are not refugee' This is an invasion, Islam entry is Death of Europe**," migrants pose threat to Europe's millennium old culture and civilization and universal values. Hungarian Prime Minister Viktor Orban has also called the flow of migrants a threat to Christian Europe and has tried to halt it, a position that other European leaders have condemned. Hungary also built razor-wire fence on its border with Serbia and Croatia ending its role of a major transit country for migrants using its land on route to northern-Europe.

Mounting social tension and political fragmentation haunts the European society, Political analysts warns it will make entire Europe less stable and crime rate will increase substantially because of immigration, how it will affect the world's most progressive and democratic European nations by vast inflow of people different in culture, attitudes, skills and economic status. Concern and fears in mind of many Europeans have grown especially since the Paris terror attacks on 13th November-2015, worried that jihadists carrying forged Syrian passports are posing as migrants in order to enter Europe and launch attacks on the Western countries.

Apprehension among Europeans that migrants pouring into Europe from Muslim dominated countries are not ordinary asylum seekers or refugees but **Multinational Islamic Army (Military)**, and will one day conquer Europe and establish **Islamic caliphate**. European observers are of the opinion that the great national cultures of Italians, French, Germans and others may be replaced by new transnational Islamic cultures and identity.

This one question is worth trillions of dollars; **"Will Islam conquer Europe and America?"**

Article title **"The invasion of Europe and America**," describes the situation; Europe on the verge to descending into utter chaos, These thousands of Muslim "refugees," most of them from the jihad hotspots of Syria, Afghanistan and Iraq, have been pouring into Greece and the Balkans in huge numbers for some time now. But they do not, of course, want to stay in Greece, Macedonia and Serbia. They want to reach the European Union: primarily Germany, France and Britain.

More of these "refugees" arrive every day. Media reports of this Muslim invasion focus on the crying women and children, who seem to have been deliberately brought to the front of the crowd. Clearly the vast majority of these "migrants" are men, and in any case, under normal circumstances, wouldn't you take the women, and especially the children, to the side so that they wouldn't get hurt in clashes with police? Instead, they are used as human shields.

Immigration jihad, or hijrah, is the migration or journey of Muhammad and his followers from Mecca to Yathrib, later renamed by him to Medina, in the year 622 CE. It was after the hijrah that Muhammad for the first time became not just a preacher of religious ideas, but a political and military leader. That was what occasioned his new "revelations" exhorting his followers to commit violence against unbelievers. Significantly, the Islamic calendar counts the hijrah, not Muhammad's birth or the occasion of his first "revelation," as the beginning of Islam, implying that Islam is not fully itself without a political and military component.

And true to that martial aspect of this immigration, the "refugees" have grown increasingly violent. Nonetheless, the enemedia and compromised government officials maintain that if you disagree with letting all these people into your country, you are a heartless hateful racist bigot. But this is as absurd as it is insidious. Imagine if this logic were applied in daily life, if someone wanted to enter your house, take all your belongings and even move in there. Should you be forced to let them in?".......

Greed becomes Good, Good becomes Bad; in 20th century world witnessed two ferociously fought World Wars, in 2nd half of 20th century as well several bloody wars were fought, Korean war, Vietnam war and Iran – Iraq war which lasted for over 8years, each of these savagely fought wars have had devastating consequences, millions of people lost their lives and millions more suffered acute humiliation and extreme economic hardship but contrary to what people at that time had feared none of these wars sparked the much anticipated 3rd WW.

But as it seems like the worse was reserve for 21st century, what started in January-2011 was initially a peoples movement in Tunisia which soon spill over to other neighbouring countries in the region to *Libya and Egypt*, **Arab Spring Revolution** (or call it **Jasmine revolution**), Arab spring revolution was something similar to 18th century French Revolution, local citizens of Tunisia and Egypt demanding greater freedom, democratic rights and accountability, Arab spring was initially a peaceful peoples movement, local citizens protesting against their respective country's dictatorial regimes, but no sooner had the peaceful Arab spring revolution had started the opportunist Islamic jihadists elements seized the opportunity and crushed the peoples movement and turned the revolutionary process into full blown Islamic Sectarian conflict, the Sunni extremist elements using oppressive measures suppressed the voice of innocent civilians who were seeking and demanding more freedom and justice for themselves in several Muslim ruled African and Arabian countries, since 2011 many Muslim dominated countries in Africa and West-Asia have plunged into deeper social and political crisis, the worst hit and most fiercely affected countries are Yemen, Syria, Libya and Iraq, also countries like Egypt, Tunisia, Nigeria, Kenya as well are among countries which have experienced terrorism, brutal terrorists perpetrating heinous crimes and violence.

Between 2011 and 2015 in several Muslim ruled countries in Arabian region and in Africa well over 400,000 people have lost their life, add couple of more Muslim ruled countries like Pakistan and Afghanistan which as well are equally seriously affected by immense terrorist activities and the count of number of deaths increases by another 20,000 at least, thousands more citizens of these violence affected nations are/were wounded with severe wounds and injuries, so much human blood has shamelessly flowed over the years, the sectarian conflict between Shia and Sunni faction of Islam and other extreme and grotesque acts of graphic violence in many Islamic countries situated in west-Asia and Africa, the terrorists activities gained further momentum since the middle of year-2014. Ever so increasing violence and killings due to civil wars and sectarian conflict between various Islamic factions and groups, with no likely possibility or chance of any kind of compromise or understanding between warring factions of Islam and hopes are fading for finding any amicable lasting peaceful solution to ever so escalating violence and atrocities in Islamic countries and worse still terrorists attacks spreading vigorously to so many other non-Muslim countries as well, therefore by the end of calendar year 2015 assessing the ground realties many political and financial analysts intensely started debating whether if the ongoing civil wars and terrorists perpetrated crimes and violence in Muslim dominated countries "was it or if it is?" an unofficial start of 3rd world war. Whether or not, the magnitude of modern terrorism threat and increase in terror attacks and beheadings of kidnapped hostages of several western countries between 2014 and 2015 can be or can't be construed as unofficial start 3rd WW, but one thing is certain that if and when and if at all, it's a big "**IF**," the 3rd world war if at all it happens will certainly will be a battle between Islam versus the rest of the world, it potentially will be "**Islam versus the rest' The Third World War.**"

Between 2011 and 2015 due to increased terrorist atrocities and continuing wars in "Syria, Yemen, Iraq and Libya" millions of citizens in these conflict-ridden and violence affected nations have been internally displaced and have lost everything they had of their own, millions of families having lost their homes and businesses, beleaguered citizens are/were forced to flee out of their respective country to seek refuge in other neighbouring countries.

While millions more have or had taken a decision to abandon their own Islamic countries all together and move to other non-Islamic countries to seek protection and shelter, according to some estimates between 2013 and 2015 at least 4.5 million people from various Muslim dominated African and Arabian countries also from Pakistan and Afghanistan have in search for peace and to find shelter have moved to safer zone and for that purpose they are or were compel to make compelling choices and taking undue risk and spending a fortune, fleeing war and poverty migrants left with no alternative had to take a tough decision to cross across the Mediterranean sea, that's how millions of migrants have entered European shore to seek refuge and asylum in prosperous west-European countries, but the small journey of crossing across the sea for these beleaguered migrants to the European shore has not been without the problems, there were horrific tragic incidents of small size overcrowded boat laden with migrants many of the ill-fated boats capsized, resulting in deaths of tens of thousands of migrants by drowning into the sea.

"*This is Real life nightmare* I must say," the political crisis as well as religious and ideological differences between various Islamic and ethnic communities in Muslim dominated countries is the worst thing happening to mankind, the so-called Arab spring revolution has indeed turned into Arab or to say Islamic nightmare.

Humanitarian crisis or humanitarian catastrophe it is arguably worse humanitarian problem since the end of 2nd world war, or in some aspect worse than that was experienced during 2nd world war. Wars and religious violence are wild and callous, most of us know that in past and perhaps even in present times in many countries and in many wars and civil wars official Army, insurgent rebels or terrorists uses **Rape as Weapon of War**, but in Syria's civil war apart from Sexual violence a new method of intimidating enemy forces have emerged, **Starvation as Weapon of War**, local citizens in many villages, towns and cities in Syria are or were being Starved, with intention to pressurize rival enemy forces and to punish supporters of political rivals and opponents, not just in Syria but there are unconfirmed reports suggest that even in some villages and cities in Iraq, Libya and Yemen same pressure tactics are or were used of cutting food and water supply with an intention to suppress opponents and to exert pressure on rival forces. Starvation is not a new weapon but a tactic from medieval times finding modern applications. As a tactic, starvation not only weakens your enemy but also places them under increasing pressure to care for civilians within the besieged site.

But as it is said, that, one problem creates many more problems, the refugee crisis in Europe is clearly humanitarian nightmare, but there is another bigger perspective to understand, the Islamic crisis and civil wars in Muslim dominated countries in west-Asia, Afghanistan, and in Africa has enveloped Europeans as well, the inrush of asylum seekers in Europe mainly from Islamic countries between 2013 and 2015, the sectarian conflict and sharp division among Muslims over their religious issues and factional feud of Islam has put European countries government officials and politicians in bizarre situation and compelled them to deal with rather unimaginable predicament.

As it is that Europe has not fully recovered from the 2008/9 global economic recession, there aren't many or rather it will be safe to assume that there are none, no new business investments particularly in manufacturing sector all over Europe, on economic front not much exciting things happening as of 2014/15 there are No new mega business investments planned for starting any big commercial industrial projects in Europe, unemployment rate as of 2014 in few prominent European countries like "Spain, Italy, Portugal and Greece was well over 15%, unemployment rate is even higher among the youths, so unemployment and underemployment is prevalent all across Europe, rising incidents of crimes, crime rate between 2004 & 2014 has risen exponentially in many key European cities. Keeping in mind abrasive ground realities, hence because of increasing flow of asylum seekers to European countries many thoughtful Rightist leaning individual people in Europe are jittery and resolutely against and unwilling to welcome migrants who are/were migrating from Islamic countries.

So to say, that bitter unending Islamic sectarian and internal religious problems have created problems within the European community as well, Islamic problems and massive flow of large number of refugees and asylum seekers from Muslim dominated countries have had brutally divided Europe into two faction, one faction inside Europe are optimists and have positive feelings for the asylum seekers and supports the idea of allowing migrants in Europe and they argue favourably for granting asylum citing reasons that the migrants from west-Asia based Islamic countries will in long term prove to be an asset and will solve chronic European demographic problems, the optimists are of the view that those migrants entering Europe have skills and talent and their talent can best be utilize for commercial purposes by European businesses, but another faction of Europeans largely consist of rightist activist and Far-Right political parties vehemently opposes any move to accommodate such large flow of millions of migrants from Muslim dominated countries, the rightists elements who opposes allowing entry to migrants are of the opinion that Muslims from Islamic countries only have one talent and that talent is **Combative terror activities and aggression**, the pessimists are arguing that in long term the Muslim refugees once they settle in Europe and consolidate their position and forms their community bases inside Europe, the crafty Islamic folks will destroy millennium old European culture and traditions and will decimate centuries old civilization.

Since the German Government between 2013 & 2015 has granted asylum to over 2 million refugees, and provided them shelter and permission to live and work in Germany, large section of mainstream German society is disgusted and annoyed with their government's **Open Door Refugee Policy**, many Germans are apprehensive because of sudden spurt in Muslim population in their country, as many in Germany fear that in long term it would have profound and devastating social and economic consequences, there is apparent fear in the minds of most Germans and also among many so-called patriotic Europeans as they fear that once the Sunni-Muslim folks establishes base of their community in Germany and France, they (Sunni-Muslims) may potentially float Boko-Haram type of jihadist terrorist outfit and those Sunni jihadists elements would wreck havoc not just in Germany but throughout Europe. Now, whether or not if this is unfounded belief and false apprehension among the Europeans or if it is a genuine concern and fear among Europeans that the Sunni Islamic folks for the purpose of Islamization of Europe would start **nasty urban guerrilla warfare** in European towns and cities and turn Germany and France into Somalia and Libya of Europe, but, another arguably the most pressing concern among the European community is that Islamic jihadists may capture young beautiful European girls and women and force them to marry jihadists or make them sex slave.

So there are/were conflicting views and split opinions among the Europeans with regards to granting asylum and to give permission to mostly Sunni-Muslim migrants from Islamic countries to settle in different prosperous European counties and earn their livelihood and their young children gets best education, so that Muslim community folks like other Europeans enjoy every basic fundamental and civil rights as per the European laws.

What has/had further harmed the Muslim community cause are/were the frequent terror attacks by the jihadi Islamist Sunni terrorists, couple of terror attacks in Tunisia killing many European tourists, couple of massive terror attacks in France and few minor but intense terror attacks in several other European countries between 2014/15, and also abrupt behaviour of young Muslim men allegedly found guilty of having Physically Abused and Sexually Assaulted young White European Women in German city of **Cologne** on New year's Eve, Muslims involvement in such barbaric crimes sparked major anti-Islam sentiments all over Europe and also in north-America,

Between 2013 & 2015, Series of terror attacks in many different countries around the world killing thousands of innocent people, --- and beheadings of several European and American nationals allegedly in Syria by inhuman Islamist Sunni jihadists, such inhumane crimes against humanity perpetrated by Muslims has made Muslim position untenable, Muslims have become unpopular and whole Islamic community particularly the Sunni-Muslims have been embarrassed and stigmatized by the acts and actions of their community members, also I would like to point out "all jihadi terrorists groups owes allegiance to Sunni Islam."

Spate of terrorist attacks in several European countries and rising incidents of crimes in European towns and cities has taken its toll on Europe's once thriving Tourism industry, millions of Chinese citizens are worth millions of U.S Dollars and have incredibly high spending and purchasing power, once Europe was most preferred holiday destination for the Chinese, millions of Chinese folks use to travel to Europe and U.S each year to spend their holidays, but sharp decline (devaluation of Yuan) in value of China's currency against major international currencies particularly the "Euro and U.S-Dollar" increases the cost of holidaying in Europe but that's only one small part of the reason, more important reason is safety concern among China's nationals, frequent terror attacks and high degree of crime rate in Europe forced many Rich Chinese to alter their annual holiday travel plans, so since middle of 2015 many Chinese did a rethink and allegedly cancelled any plan if at all they had of spending their holidays in Europe or even in other troubled mainstream tourist destination of the world which apparently are not too far away from shores of Europe countries like Turkey, Egypt and Tunisia, and instead Chinese opts to travel to more safer countries in Asia. While supper rich Chinese prefers to travel to Japan, New Zealand and Australia to spend holidays, the middle-income folks from China prefers to travel to countries like Thailand, Dubai, Indonesia and South-Africa to spend leisure holidays, thereby massively hurting business interest of Europeans as well also of the troubled Islamic countries like "Tunisia, Egypt and Turkey" which as well are considered unsafe due to increase terror attacks and rampant fear of Sunni jihadist terrorists. But not only the Chinese even the rich and wealthy Asian Muslims as well instead of Europe they prefer to spend their leisure holidays in countries like Malaysia, Thailand, Singapore and or in Dubai. So if Europe and Egypt are losing business others like Australia and Malaysia etc are gaining, as there is a saying, "One man's misfortune is an opportunity for another man."

If we are discussing 21st century humanitarian crisis and of Europe's political and economic crisis then it is also important for us to understand little bit of past Europe's history as well, here I would like to share an interesting Article title **"Political Situation in Europe on the Eve of French Revolution,"** "On the eve of the French Revolution the political situation in Europe was remarkably simple. The Continent was dominated by five great powers: Britain, France, Austria, Russia, and Prussia. Their neighbors – Spain, Sweden, and Turkey – had all once enjoyed periods of economic, military, or naval greatness, but by the end of the 18th century had slipped into the ranks of the lesser powers. Most of western Germany remained fragmented into hundreds of minor principalities, ecclesiastical cities, and minor states contained within the Holy Roman Empire. Italy, similarly, contained a number of small kingdoms, some independent and others controlled by

Austria. Europe was overwhelmingly agrarian and feudal, particularly in the east, with monarchs ruling absolutely within their domains. Britain was a somewhat different case: though the vast majority of her people were disenfranchised, the monarchy ruled under constitutional constraints. The nation's prosperity was based not on agriculture but on trade. The process of industrialization, though still in its infancy, was well under way.

A generation before the French Revolution, Prussia, under the ruling house of Hohenzollern, had established herself as Europe's newest great power, having won a series of costly and exhausting wars in which she had taken on and defeated practically every major state on the Continent. Frederick the Great had inherited from his father, Frederick William (1713-40), a highly militarized, extremely efficient state where the landed aristocracy and king enjoyed a close relationship. The aristocracy were freeholders of their land and, in effect, over their peasants as well. In return, the crown taxed the nation heavily in order to maintain a standing army proportionally much larger than that of any other European state. Frederick used that army aggressively: he invaded Austrian Silesia in 1740, and thus began the War of the Austrian Succession (1740-48). This was followed by the Seven Years' War (1756-63) (see Osprey Essential Histories, The Seven Years' War, by Daniel Marston) in which Prussia used her formidable army for the glory of the nation and to consolidate her territorial gains, generally at the expense of Austria. During the Seven Years' War Frederick fought the greatest coalition ever seen in Europe – Austria, France, Russia, Sweden, and most of the German states of the Holy Roman Empire – and survived intact. It was the hard-fought bloody encounters of this war that confirmed for Prussia her place among the Great Powers.

The Russian Empire covered a vast stretch of territory containing at the turn of the century about 48 million subjects, over half of whom were serfs tied to the land. The autocratic Romanov dynasty had ruled since the early 17th century. Russia's military reputation had been won under Peter the Great, who had defeated the Swedes in the Great Northern War (1700-21). Although Russia had briefly fought Prussia in the later years of the Seven Years' War, her territorial gains were made at Polish and Turkish expense during the reign of Catherine the Great (1762-96), particularly during the First Partition of Poland in 1772 and in the annexation of the Crimea, an Ottoman possession, in 1783. Russia fought simultaneous conflicts with Sweden (1788-90) and, in alliance with Austria, Turkey (1787-92). She was ultimately successful in both of these conflicts. When the French Revolutionary Wars began, Catherine the Great remained neutral and she died four years later in 1796 without having challenged the Revolution. That task was left to her son and successor, Paul I, who would finally face France during the War of the Second Coalition (1798-1802). Paul was known for his mental instability and obsession with military matters and was assassinated in 1801.

George III, who had presided over the somewhat different and more constitutional monarchy of Britain since 1760, proved to be one of the French Revolution's most implacable opponents. Political power rested with Parliament and the Prime Minister. William Pitt the Younger had attained office in 1783 with a loyal following in the House of Commons and the support of the crown. Though small by continental standards – with a population of fewer than 10 million – Britain was the world's most prosperous nation. Her wealth was based on thriving trade with Europe and her exclusive access to a vast empire which, in addition to Canada and, above all, India, included newly acquired territories in Australia and many of the bountiful "sugar islands" of the West Indies. As international trade was the basis of the rapidly increasing national wealth, the protection of trade was paramount. Britain's unrivalled merchant fleet, which exceeded 10,000 vessels, could confidently rely on the power of the Royal Navy for its protection. Although agriculture was still important – accounting for one-third of the national product – Britain was the birthplace of the recent phenomenon of industrialization, and its growing manufacturing capacity played a major role in stimulating a booming economy. Britain and France were long-standing enemies, having fought one another regularly over the past century and on opposite sides in nearly every conflict in which the two countries were engaged since the Middle Ages."……..

These are defining moments, I call it evolving situation! Conflicting views and varied opinions, selfish motives and purposes, internal rift and confusion among European politicians over drafting more acceptable "European immigration policy," the humanitarian crisis is/was far more severe in 2015/16 than it was in 1945/46 after the end of 2nd WW.

Like many people in Germany and in central Europe in the 1920s and 1930s had a perception, who believed their Race or racial group the **"Aryan Race"** is supreme and better than every other Human Race, arrogant as they were, the so-called people of Aryan race allegedly used to despise every other Racial groups and use to consider every other human Race as inferior and use to say that only their 'Aryan Race' is the Master Race, on similar line like the rightists elements once in Germany and some other parts of Europe firmly believed in their Race "Aryan" as Master Race. The Sunni Muslims outrageously have unofficially declared that there Religious Faith the "Sunni Islam' is a' Master Religion" better than every other religious belief and every other religion and non-believers are inferior, so much selfishness that the conceit Sunni Muslim folks without any hesitation calls every Non-Sunni Muslim people Infidel and infidels according to Sunni Islam doctrine are considered as evil, thus disrespecting and harming the non-Muslims in any possible manner is not considered sin but holy duty of every Sunni-Muslim.

The gulf between Islam and all the other religious communities and ideologies is ever so widening, social, cultural and economic divide, what many intellectuals perceive as incredibly dangerous sign of things that may potentially unravel in coming years and decades, which ultimately would prove to become an end game of human's survival on this wonderful planet Earth.

The people from various different religion and non-believers who detest Islam for obvious reasons, normally, they are seen sinking their differences and uniting to oppose the diktat of Islam and of its followers (Muslims) as vigorously as possible, the strong dislike and discontent among masses against the brutality of Islam, to some extent unites them to at least to oppose and talk against the savage crimes committed by Islam and atrocities committed by its followers, but conflict of interest and selfish commercial interest of non-Islamic people and communities have failed so far in evolving any comprehensive and decisive policy to defeat the objectives of the "arrogant followers" of Islamic faith. The *war on terror* started in 2001 against the Sunni Muslim jihadist terrorist groups so far has/have proved futile, it has only resulted in loss of money and lives.

The followers of Islam have time and again have made their intentions clear, that, they are united among themselves and unambiguously moving ahead with a clear motive to destroy whatever is non Islamic and against the very ethics and principle of Islam.

Allah is the name of Islamic God, and the followers of Islam are thought right from their childhood, that, there is no God accept one and only Allah (the name of Muslim God), and that prophet Mohammed (the founder of Islam) is slave of Allah and rest (all Muslims) are slave of prophet Mohammed, every Muslim is made to believe that almighty Allah sent their Prophet Mohammed to the world with a message of peace and as a messenger of god to spread the belief and words of Allah.

Allah is supreme god and prophet Mohammed is his messenger, so all who love and believe in teachings of Mohammed that person/persons is/are the true believers of Allah, rest of the people in this world who do not accept and embrace Islam and pledge allegiance to their prophet Mohammed, those individual peoples and communities are considered by Muslims as non-believers and without any remorse or hesitancy the Muslims particularly the Sunni Muslims call such people Infidels and considers non-believers as Satan (evil).

Muslims are adaptive and change their mood and attributes as per the situation, if humble approach doesn't work than they adopt aggressive approach, Sunni-Muslim population growth is both organic and inorganic, early marriages and high birth rates among Muslims especially Sunnis, but, Islamic religious organizations also wants as many as possible non-Muslims convert to Islam to strengthen their numerical strength and their unholy plan is to reduce other religious communities to minority, earlier the Sunnis use to use strong arm measures such as Violence, killings and rape to force non-Muslim folks to convert to Islam, in modern times Muslims have adopted more humble approach and instead of aggression Islamists tries to lure non-Muslims to convert to Islam by persuasion, sweet talking and helpful nature, non-Muslims conversion to Islam helps Islamic causes, as it helps Islam win battle against Christianity and various pagan religions. Prison cells of European countries be it in U.K., France or Netherlands even across the Atlantic ocean in U.S. and Canada, prison is where all evil come together, Islamic clerics or other petty criminals serving jail sentence volunteers themselves for their religion (Islam) cause, Muslim prisoners gets an exciting opportunity to mingle with lots of other non-Muslim folks inside the prison, therefore they take full advantage of this opportunity and befriends as many non-Muslim inmates inside jail, spends long time chatting and socializing with them and systematically preaches them Koranic verses (Islam holy-book) and distributes other toxic literature to non-Muslim prisoners which glorifies Islam and Allah (name of Islamic god) and demonizes other religions, this is how selfish Sunni Islamists indoctrinates and brainwashes mind of non-Muslims and systematically forces them to embrace Islam and pledge allegiance to their "**prophet Muhammed**," so prisons in Europe and America are the places where maximum conversion happens. Younger demographic are particularly vulnerable, in schools and universities Muslim youths exploits young non-Muslim girls and seduce them force them to marry them, also preaches them Islam to make them understand the benefits of embracing Islam.

Muslim-Brotherhood and Islam jihadi army strategists in their bid to conquer Europe are particularly harsh on Europe's most glamourous country "**France**," knowing well the significance of France and how much important it is for jihadists forces to weaken France so as to gain full economic and political control of Europe and subsequently conquer America and establish Sharia rule (Islamic religious law). Germany may be largest country in Europe and global economic power-house, but, France is the only country in continental Europe that have tremendous military power and is heavily nuclear armed nation, French military and security forces are one of the best in the world, France have great superiority in both Air and ground defence and combat, with high-powered weaponry and Fighter-aircrafts that can tear enemy/enemies apart, therefore Islamist strategists are fully concentrated to sabotage France from within, instil fear in minds of French people, refugees from Islamic countries as well as local Muslims staying in France constantly harass mainstream French community in many different cities, it is alleged miscreants Muslim youngsters frequently indulges in violent arguments, street corner fights and tiff with French people at public places and parks and tourist spots, besides, between 2015 and 2016 jihadists have unleash terror, several deadly terror attacks and dozens of minor but brutal lone-wolf attacks killing or seriously injuring innocent people. The purpose behind such high degree of crimes perpetrated by the Islamists is to destabilize France. Creating social problems, political instability and economic uncertainty will cripple France, once France "**falls**" that will clear the way and remove all obstacle for the selfish Islamic jihadi army to conquer Europe as no other European nation including Germany has the capacity or tenacity to fight and to defeat Islamic jihadi army, jihadists are formidable force, they are well trained to fight urban guerrilla warfare.

Muslim Brotherhood was formed in 1928 by an Egyptian **Hassan al-Banna** as an Islamist Political and Social movement, after the humiliating defeat and near total decimation of the than powerful **ottoman empire** after the 1st world-war in 1918, Muslim Brotherhood was formed obviously for Sunni Islamic causes, to spread Islam and Koranic studies and determined to establish Sharia law (Islam religious rule) worldwide, Muslim brotherhood is tremendously powerful organization with vast resources and highly talented people working for it, all the major Sunni Islam criminal gangs and terror groups are inextricably linked with Muslim-brotherhood, the strategy of Sunni institution is simple, create problems in Islamic countries, orchestrate religious wars and violence so that it provides valid reasons for Muslims to migrate to non-Muslim countries, infiltrate non-Muslim ruled countries and grow Muslim population as much as possible which apparently will help Islam conquer the world, without ever fighting more conventional wars out in the open battlefields.

Article title "**Muslim invasion of Europe**" writes, "The flow of illegal migrants does not stop. They land on the Greek islands along the Turkish coast. They still try to get into Hungary, despite a razor wire fence and mobilized army. Their destination is Germany or Scandinavia, sometimes France or the UK. Some of them still arrive from Libya. Since the beginning of January, more than 620,000 have arrived by sea alone. There will undoubtedly be many more: a leaked secret document estimates that by the end of December, there might be 1.5 million.

Journalists in Western Europe continue to depict them as "refugees" fleeing war in Syria. The description is false. According to statistics released by the European Union, only twenty-five percent of them come from Syria; the true number is probably lower. The Syrian government sells passports and birth certificates at affordable prices. The vast majority of migrants come from other countries: Iraq, Afghanistan, Pakistan, Eritrea, Somalia, and Nigeria.

Many do not seem to have left in a hurry. Many bring new high-end smartphones and large sums of cash, ten or twenty thousand euros, sometimes more. Many have no passports, no ID, and refuse to give fingerprints.

- The sudden arrival of hundreds of thousands more Muslims most likely prompts Europeans to think that the nightmare will get worse; they see, powerlessly, that their leaders speak and act as if they have no awareness of what is happening.

- Central European leaders and people, who have already lived under authoritarian rule, seem to be thinking that entering the European Union was a huge mistake. They came to what was then called the "free world." They do not seem willing to be subjected again to coercive decisions made by outsiders.
- Illegal Muslim migrants will live on social benefits until the bankruptcy of welfare states.
- In all 28 countries of the European Union, birth rates are low and the population is aging. People under thirty account for only 16% of the population, or 80 million people. In the 22 Arab countries, plus Turkey and Iran, people under thirty account for 70% of the population, or 350 million people.".............

When Benedict XVI visited Turkey, his main purpose was to meet with Bartholomew I, the ecumenical patriarch of Constantinople and the spiritual leader of 300 million Eastern Orthodox. For a millennium Constantinople was the seat of a thriving empire. It was conquered by Muslims in 1453 and renamed Istanbul. Today Bartholomew reigns over a few buildings and fewer than 3,000 Turkish Christians. The patriarchate exists at the sufferance of the Turkish government and with the reluctant acquiescence of the imams.

Imagine a similar future for the Church of Rome. Imagine, a few generations from now, that Europeans have failed to reproduce themselves and have failed to resuscitate their faith. If present trends continue, in some European countries fully half of the population will be Muslim not long after mid-century. At some point *sharia* will be introduced. Historical legal structures, such as British common law and the Code Napoleon, will give way to the law of the Qu'ran. Year by year the Christian minority will become ever more isolated.

The "rape game" Taharrush is about a large group of Arab men surrounding their victim, usually a Western woman or a woman wearing Western-style clothing, and then the women are subjected to sexual abuse. They surround the victim in circles. The men in the inner circle are the ones who physically abuse the woman, the next circle are the spectators, while the mission of the third circle is to distract and divert attention to what's going on.

If there is enough men, the woman is dragged along by the mob, while the men take turns ripping her clothes off, grope her, and inserting fingers in her various body orifices. Taharrush is noted in Egypt as a kind of "lighter sexual abuse or gang rape" and occurred during the Egyptian Revolution (The Arab Spring) of 2011 in the unrest at the Tahrir Square, where Egyptian women and in some cases foreign journalists were surrounded by groups of men, often having been touched with sexual intent and partly undressed, stripped naked and gang raped. There need not be much overt persecution. An effete population will be disinclined to resist the changes. There will be many opportunistic conversions to Islam. High Muslim birth rates and much-increased Muslim immigration will see to it that Christians become numerically inconsequential. They will be permitted to practice their faith, so long as they do so quietly.

Many point to the rapes in Tahrir Square (in' Cairo) in 2011 and 2013 as cautionary tales, describing the so-called "circle of hell" that women faced then: lone women surrounded by men whose hands groped and pulled, ripped and pressed, and eventually overpowered. A 2013 study conducted after the attacks showed that a stunning 99 percent of Egyptian women had experienced some sort of sexual harassment.

True, these asylum-seekers are not Egyptian, but the signs were there all along. And despite new crackdowns on male asylum-seeker from the region, the problem is likely to continue so long as conservative Muslim men remain among their ranks, finding their way into European cities as new citizens. Observed Brenda Stoter, a reporter and sociologist who has spent several years covering women in the region for Al Jazeera and Dutch newspaper *De Groene,* in a recent essay, "Anyone who thinks that you can bring the Arabic world to Europe without social inequality, cultural differences, and the influence of religion, ignores the facts."…..

Sunni-Muslims have problems with everything, they've problems with "Beer, wine, bikini clad girls, women wearing skimpy clothes like short frock, nightclubs and discos, all types of music, artefacts, they dislike Jewish community, they hate atheists and detest gays and lesbians, in super-markets they want Halal food, in cosmetic shops they want Halal (legitimate as per Islamic law permitted by Sharia) cosmetic items Perfumes and lipsticks without any alcohol, pork or blood contains, in airlines while travelling they (Muslims) insist Halal food is served to them, they want prayer hall or some kind of adjustment be made so as to offer their regular prayers at workplace or you'll see them praying right on street pavement or on the corner of the road or in case while travelling they pray on railway platform or at airport lounge," damn it these Muslims are so demanding and fussy want preferential treatments and privileges, irrespective and regardless of which country they are in or live in, no matter where they are, they want everything as per their religion's permissible rule, if their religion 'Islam' restricts them from so many things, than for "what purpose do these Muslims migrate to non-believers progressive European and American countries? Why can't Muslims live as per their traditions in their own respective Islamic countries and do what they like best doing? And allow the rest of the world's non-Muslim population live in peace. Sunni-Muslims desirously find peace in destroying other people's peace.

Outlining the fundamental differences between eastern Islam and western Christianity — "culture, architecture, music, gastronomy, dress" — the editorial explains these two worlds have been at war "over the last 14 centuries" and the world is now witnessing a colossal "clash of two civilisations in the countries of old Europe". This clash is brought by Muslims who come to Europe and "carry conflict with the Western world as part of the collective consciousness", as the journalist marks the inevitability of conflict between native Europeans and their new guests. The narrative of an Islamic or Arab takeover of Europe, though hardly new, has gained real traction in recent months, propagated by both xenophobic activist groups as well as populist political leaders and parties. Differences of opinion are being sought to be settled by using physical violence. Arguments are met not with counter arguments but with bullets, To be sure, there are legitimate security concerns posed both by the surge in new arrivals as well as the continuing instability and conflicts in the Middle East.

In several Islamic countries most notoriously in Pakistan "**Blasphemy laws**" are used by Islamic extremists to make up charges against innocent Hindus and Christians in order to steal their property and stir up violence against the Christian population. This includes cases of abduction of women, rape and forced marriages.

Estimated to be five million, the Muslim population in USA as of 2015 is about the size of the Hispanic population 27 years ago, but it is growing six times faster than the national rate, thanks to high rates of birth, immigration and conversions. Many African-Americans view Christianity as the White man's religion and associate conversion to Islam with recovering their ethnic heritage. Thus, to effectively evangelize African-American Muslims. The first actual African-American Muslim sect was the Moorish Science Temple Divine and National Movement of North America, founded in Newark, New Jersey by Timothy Drew (Noble Drew Ali) in 1913. In 1925, the name of the sect was changed to the Moorish Temple of Science. Drew Ali developed the 'Koran of the Moorish Holy Temple of Science' and taught that Allah had ordained him as his prophet to the dark people of America. Ali stated that Negro and Black signified death and Coloured signified something painted. Therefore, the terms Asiatic, Moor or Moorish-American must be used. Ali taught that salvation was found by discovering national origin and refusing to be called Negro, Black, Coloured, Ethiopian, etc. Many converts feel uncomfortable with the term "black Muslim", as they regard themselves as part of a worldwide community of believers who do not recognize "race." However, others are less reticent about associating their blackness with being a Muslim, and believe that **Islam** is the "natural religion of black people" and provides the means for full "spiritual, mental and physical liberation" from an oppressive system designed to subjugate them. The tendency by many in the West to bury their heads in the sand and wish away the reality is driven by fear, unpreparedness for and unwillingness to pay the price that this war will require, as well as general fatigue and distaste for conflict after over a decade of it in Iraq and Afghanistan. The **Organization of Islamic Cooperation** is the largest and most powerful voting bloc in the United Nations and yet most Americans have never heard of it. Of particular concern is the OIC's ten-year program which amounts to an international effort to suppress freedom of expression under the guise of protecting Islam from so-called "defamation." This initiative, however, is in the service of OIC's long-term mission: the world-wide implementation of **Sharia**, a legal-political-judicial-religious doctrine which favours Muslims over non-Muslims, men over women, and denies basic human rights and freedoms. As practiced today, the **Hijra** strategy is an important part of a covert, *pre*-violent "civilization jihad" pursued by the Muslim Brotherhood. The UN High Commission on Refugees – which, like the rest of the United Nations, is dominated by the dictates of the Islamic supremacist organization known as the Organization of Islamic Cooperation (OIC) – is complicit in the process of bringing Muslim refugees to America. Interestingly, no Muslim refugees are ever resettled in wealthy, low-population density Islamic countries like Saudi Arabia.

"**Jamaat al Fuqra**" is an alleged Pakistani Islamic group responsible for a string of **murders, bombings** and other terrorist acts across the world, including in the USA. Its chapter in America calls itself, "**Muslims of America**" (**MOA**), and actively recruits at **mosques** and prisons, where African-American inmates are especially targeted. Islamization of America is accelerating. In tandem with the spread of **Sharia law in America**'s courts, In the Western countries, few Islamic imams openly preach Jihad - Islam's "holy" war - against us (western civilization). But to Muslim-only audiences, imams do preach waging war against non-Muslims. In some Islam-penetrated Western nations like the UK, imams have begun to throw off the cloak of **Taqiyya** and openly declare war against unbelievers in western nations, even on live television. Islamization of the American media, political and education systems in particular is gaining momentum and confidence, and there is near unanimity that it will continue.

Do **CAIR** (Council on American Islamic Relations) and other activist groups merely want to support Black Lives Matter, or do they hope to recruit blacks to their own cause? In 2014, ISIS used the protests and clashes in Ferguson, Missouri as an opportunity to attempt to **recruit blacks** to radical Islam. But ISIS is a known terrorist organization while CAIR, despite its shady history, is considered by many to be a moderate, mainstream Muslim organization. Thus, if it wanted to convert blacks, it would presumably want to convert them to a moderate version of Islam.

Will Islam catch on with black Americans? A great many blacks in America have a strong commitment to Christianity, which serves to act as a buffer against conversion to Islam. Still, it's likely that Islam will make more inroads into the black community than it has in the past. For one thing, traditional Islam doesn't have the "kook" factor which keeps most blacks at a distance from The Nation of Islam. The NOI belief system includes giant space ships, an evil scientist who created a race of "white devils," and, most recently, an embrace of Dianetics.

Even more troubling, Islamic groups, including **Muslim Brotherhood's** Council on American Islamic Relations (**CAIR**), have penetrated the highest levels of the U.S. government. The White House now has a White House Muslim Advisor, who has counterpart Muslim advisors at the U.S. Department of Justice, the FBI, and the U.S. Department of Homeland Security, where Senior Fellow, **Mohamed Elibiary** declared that USA is an "Islamic country." Much of the money for building mosques, Islamic schools and other Muslim assets in the West comes from the oil rich Muslim nations in the Middle East. And they get their money from the West by selling petroleum oil and gas to European and Americans. Saudi Arabia alone raked in $256 billion from oil exports, and a bulk of that money then was funnelled back out to the West via groups like the **Muslim Brotherhood's** North American Islamic Trust (**NAIT**) to build and own Islamic assets. Not only have Muslims declared war against us: they already are waging it, burning churches, beheading and/or massacring Christians in Iraq, Syria, Ethiopia, Egypt, Saudi Arabia, Pakistan, Sudan, Somalia, Iran, Nigeria, Yemen, Kenya, Indonesia, Turkey, Afghanistan, Eritrea, Iraq, Bangladesh, Malaysia, Mali, etc.

Black lives matter movement gaining momentum in America, in a similar manner like the "**Arab spring revolutionary movement**" of 2011, "Violent and stealth" Jihadis will use any and every opportunity to gain ground. They are particularly "good" at soliciting and manipulating angry youth – from every class and race – who are misfits or underdogs looking for a sense of purpose and personal power. "Arab Spring" revolutions which were inspired by the Muslim Brotherhood and which brought death and destruction to wide swaths of the Middle East and North Africa.

The move to bring black Americans into the Islamic fold actually predates CAIR and ISIS by quite a few generations. Black Muslim organizations such as Louis Farrakhan's The Nation of Islam have been recruiting blacks to their unorthodox brand of Islam for decades. The vast majority of blacks have resisted the temptation to join, perhaps because of NOI's overt racism, its anti-Semitism, and its criticism of Christianity.

Article title "**Bringing to the life Islamic History of Europe**" has written; "Chronicling the Islamic influence on modern Europe, this evocative film brings to life a time when emirs and caliphs dominated Spain and Sicily and Islamic scholarship swept into the major cities of Europe. The journey thus recreated reveals the debt owed to Islam for its vital contribution to the European Renaissance. The film revisits Spain, Sicily and France in search of the story of Islam in Europe, uncovering an incredible tale of scientific advances and rich cultural influences. To many, East and West appear set on an inevitable collision course, with Christianity, Judaism and Islam locked in permanent confrontation. But on this revealing journey through the common past of Islam and Europe, Rageh Omaar, who came to international attention for his moving accounts of the Iraq war, proves that this is not how it has always been.

Armed with his special insight and knowledge of the Middle East, Rageh sets out from the coast of southern Spain where Muslims first entered the Iberian Peninsula in 711 CE. He travels to Cordoba where he discovers a city once ruled by Muslims that was centuries ahead of any in Europe. Medieval Cordobans trod pavements lit up by street lamps; it would be hundreds of years before Londoners and Parisians no longer wallowed in mud through darkened streets.

From there his journey continues to 13th century Paris, where Christian scholars were persecuted by the Church for trying to apply logic to religious faith. The battle was sparked by the writings of Averroes, a Muslim philosopher from Cordoba whose incisive readings of Aristotle (about what was truth and what was revelation) aroused controversy in Paris and helped launch Western secular enquiry 300 years before the Renaissance, establishing Paris as the intellectual centre of Europe for centuries to come.

Back in Spain, while this intellectual crisis was breaking in Paris, the Nastrid Dynasty of Granada was building what would be the last will and testament to Muslim rule in the West.

Inside the magnificent royal palaces of the Alhambra, Rageh gets to see at first hand the knowledge Muslims possessed in mathematics, architecture and poetry. But in 1492, the year Christopher Columbus set sail for the new world, Muslims lost their last kingdom in medieval Europe to Spain's first monarchs, Ferdinand and Isabella.".........

Extremely conservative Islamic religious hierarchy and also many of the so-called moderates Muslims considers western education as well as western lifestyle as imperialist, because they feel it has influence of Zionist Christian and Zionist Jewish culture and religion which could potentially prove harmful to Islam and to its followers, therefore it is no secret that we see it on social media as well on mainstream media the fanatic Islamic clerics trying to persuade and restrain Muslims particularly the Sunni Muslim folks from going to Christian missionaries manage Schools and universities because it is term as Haraam (illegitimate) according to Islamic jurisprudence and against the Sharia (Islamic religious law).

Now the fundamentalist Muslims may in public protest western type lifestyles and western education, they may curse the progress and development of modern science, Ironically each and every of the Islamic Sunni jihadist terror groups (Islam holy warrior) makes optimal use of modern day and time science and technology, the terrorist can't survive without modern mass communication systems, so they vigorously use more contemporary social media network which helps them immensely in spreading message and propagating barbaric Islamic propaganda, the jihadist Sunni Muslim militants makes extensive use of modern communication devices which are the technological products which apparently are researched & developed largely by scientist and technicians belonging Jewish community, also, when Muslims are sick or injured to cure sickness and to heal injuries they consume medicine which are most likely to be researched and developed by those individual scientist and doctors who by faith or by belief maybe either Jewish or maybe even atheist and non-believers and most likely be made and manufactured in Jewish or Christian owned factories, so these are some of the prime examples which proves how brazen double standards this Islamic people have.

Article title **"The true history of Europe and Islam"** describes; "The true story of Christendom and Islam is the antithesis of such claims. Consider some facts for a moment:

A mere decade after the birth of Islam in the 7th century, the jihad burst out of Arabia. Leaving aside all the thousands of miles of ancient lands and civilizations that were permanently conquered -- including Morocco, Algeria, Tunisia, Libya, Egypt, Syria, Iraq, Iran, and parts of India and China -- much of Europe was also, at one time or another, conquered by the sword of Islam.

Among other nations and territories that were attacked and/or came under Muslim domination are (to give them their modern names in no particular order): Portugal, Spain, France, Italy, Sicily, Switzerland, Austria, Hungary, Greece, Russia, Poland, Bulgaria, Ukraine, Lithuania, Romania, Albania, Serbia, Armenia, Georgia, Crete, Cyprus, Croatia, Bosnia-Herzegovina, Macedonia, Belarus, Malta, Sardinia, Moldova, Slovakia, and Montenegro.

In 846, Rome was sacked and the Vatican defiled by Muslim Arab raiders; some 600 years later, in 1453, Christendom's other great basilica, Holy Wisdom (or Hagia Sophia) was conquered by Muslim Turks, permanently. (Till this day, Turkish Muslims celebrate the sack of Constantinople, which saw much rapine and slaughter.)The few European regions that escaped direct Islamic occupation due to their northwest remoteness include Great Britain, Scandinavia, and Germany.

That, of course, does not mean that they were not attacked by Islam. Indeed, in the furthest northwest of Europe, in Iceland, Christians used to pray that God save them from the "terror of the Turk." This was not mere paranoia; as late as 1627, Muslim corsairs raided the northern Christian island seizing four hundred captives and selling them in the slave markets of Algiers.

Nor did America escape. A few years after the formation of the United States, in 1800, American trading ships in the Mediterranean were plundered and their sailors enslaved by Muslim corsairs.

The ambassador of Tripoli explained to Thomas Jefferson that it was a Muslim's "right and duty to make war upon them [non-Muslims] wherever they could be found, and to enslave as many as they could take as prisoners."

In short, for roughly one millennium -- punctuated by a Crusader-rebuttal that the modern West is obsessed with demonizing -- Islam daily posed an existential threat to Christian Europe and by extension Western civilization.

And therein lies the rub: Today, whether as taught in high school or graduate school, whether as portrayed by Hollywood or the news media, the predominant historical narrative is that Muslims are the historic "victims" of "intolerant" Western Christians. (**Watch my response** to a Fox News host wondering why Christians have always persecuted Muslims.)

So here we are, paying the price of being an ahistorical society: A few years after the Islamic strikes of 9/11 -- merely the latest in the centuries-long, continents-wide jihad on the West -- Americans elected (twice) a man with a Muslim name and heritage for president; a man who condemns the Crusades while **openly empowering the same Islamic ideology that European Christians fought for centuries**.

Surely the United States' European forebears -- who at one time or another either fought off or were conquered by Islam -- must be turning in their graves.

But all this is history, you say? Why rehash it? Why not let it be and move on, begin a new chapter of mutual tolerance and respect, even if history must be "touched up" a bit?

This would be a somewhat plausible position -- if not for the fact that, all around the globe, Muslims are *still* exhibiting the same **imperial impulse** and **intolerant supremacism** that their conquering forbears did. The only difference is that the Muslim world is currently incapable of defeating the West through a conventional war.

Yet this may not even be necessary. Thanks to the West's ignorance of history, some Muslims are flooding Europe under the guise of "immigration," refusing to assimilate, and forming enclaves which in modern parlance are called "ghettoes" but in Islamic terminology are the *ribat* -- frontier posts where the jihad is wage'd on the infidel, one way or the other.

All this leads to another, perhaps even more important point: If the true history of the West and Islam is being turned upside its head, what other historical "orthodoxies" being peddled around as truth are also false?

Were the Dark Ages truly benighted because of the "suffocating" forces of Christianity? Or were these dark ages -- which "coincidentally" occurred during the same centuries when jihad was constantly harrying Europe -- a product of another suffocating "religion"?

Was the Spanish Inquisition -- also condemned by Obama -- a reflection of Christian barbarism or was it a reflection of Christian desperation vis-à-vis the many Muslims who, while claiming to have converted to Christianity, were practicing taqiyya and living as moles trying to subvert the Christian nation back to Islam?

Don't expect to get true answers to these and other questions from the makers, guardians, and disseminators of the West's fabricated epistemology.

In the future (whatever one there may be) the histories written about our times will likely stress how our era, ironically called the "information age," was not an age when people were so well informed, but rather an age when disinformation was so widespread and unquestioned that generations of people lived in bubbles of alternate realities -- till they were finally popped."............

They (Sunni-Muslims) don't even respect the non-Muslims dead souls, in one of the incident in Libya, it was reported, Armed vandals attacked and smashed the headstones of Allied and Italian service members laid to rest in a World War II cemetery in Benghazi and then posted video of their desecration online. The U.K. Foreign Office said that on February 24 and 26 (2016) hundreds of headstones in two British military cemeteries in Benghazi were vandalized. Markers identifying Christian or Jewish war dead were damaged or broken. In video re-posted on YouTube the men (including the videographer) are seen kicking over or smashing headstones. One man takes a hammer to a ceremonial Cross of Remembrance. Men are heard saying of the dead, "They are dogs."

When Muslims from Asia or Africa migrates in search for better lifestyle and to find better job and business opportunities to the most progressive nations of the world to countries such as Australia, New Zealand, U.S., Canada, or any west-European countries, with regards to immigrant Muslims, how are Muslims treated? Are Muslim folks well accepted among local citizens of developed countries? Do Muslim immigrants respect the sentiments of local people, are they law abiding? This are some of the most pressing questions that comes to the mind of many of us, are Muslims an asset or a liability for the country they migrate too, or are the Muslims painful Scums, the answer and replies from most people will be that Muslims are liability and scums, they demand too much but contributes too little.

Most obvious fact, that, the Muslims and particularly the Sunni-Muslim folks can't change their religious attributes and cannot ever get rid of their insular beliefs, they find it always difficult to socio-culturally blend themselves among other cultures and civilizations, once the Sunni-Muslims forms a group and community union in whichever country they are in, they will unitedly mess up with others, not all but most Muslims will seldom adopt other non-Islamic cultural characteristics and will always hesitate in appreciating other religions culture and traditions, instead most Muslims with whimsical sense of humour will try to force their barbaric chemistry on others.

The Muslims especially the Sunni-Muslims are always in haste to expand their religion's base and to enhance numerical strength, for fulfilling their purpose, wherever they go they will setup Islamic religious centres and will start preaching their religious theology, they'll lure and systematically pressurise non-Muslim individuals to convert to Islam. Muslims are good at bragging and exaggerating.

Whether the Muslims are in U.S., U.K. or Australia they will protest and demand special privileges for their community, they want Food and beverages, clothes and cosmetic as per their religious doctrine, which means items needs to be Halal (legitimate according to Islamic doctrine), what is not served to Muslims as per their religious rule is called Haraam (illegitimate), Muslims will demand food be cooked and prepared as per "permissible and lawful" means according to Islamic rules or else their sentiments are hurt, they want food serve as per Islamic permissible rules even in the Airlines they are flying in irrespective of the fact whether if the airline is owned by Muslim or non-Muslim countries, which means other fellow passengers are left with no choice but eat food as per the Islamic peoples choices.

Muslims have issues with almost everything, not only they want their own women to follow strict Islamic dress code but they will also have issues with women of other religions dresses as well, Muslims also objects to nightclubs and discos, Muslim folks will object to having any shop selling alcohol or Pork meat in their area.

Muslims are disliked by most because of their behavioural attitude, which is a proven fact, they are rather more ruthless and selfish, while Muslims are extremely possessive and take utmost care in protecting the dignity of their own women, but the Male Muslim folks have indifferent attitude and style of dealing with non-Muslim especially the Non-Sunni females. Most of the stereotypes Sunni-Muslim men have prejudice and believe that flirting and seducing non-Sunni Muslim females is their birth right, even the Sunni-Muslim cleric and priest have allegedly express their view that it is **Ok** for Sunni-Muslim young men to seduce, flirt, marry do anything they like with non-Sunni Muslim females, it will not be considered as sin, because of Sunni Muslim perception that every non-Sunni Muslims are infidels and according to Sunni-Islam doctrine harming the interest of infidels (non-Sunni Muslims & non-believers) in any possible manner is considered as their holy duty (Muslim considers the infidels as evil).

Called as "**Romeos of terror**," various crime investigation team in U.K. have discovered that for decades several group of savage Muslim men mainly from south-Asia have been luring young girls, the girls are mostly teenage White European girls but it has been discovered and found that not just white-English girls but even Hindu and Sikh community girls are lured with money and Drugs and systematically seduced and raped than sexually exploited, some of the U.K. based Sikh girls complain that Pakistani Muslim men woo them seduce them when they become pregnant they compel beleaguered girls to convert to Islam and marry them, in few confessional statement it is also alleged that these monsters mostly Pakistani Muslim men after marriage took their wives to Pakistan than allegedly have sold the Hindu and Sikh girls to prostitution rackets in Pakistan.

The same story of cruelty is displayed in every other parts of Europe by immigrant Muslims, in Sweden the immigrant Muslim population is just 5%, but this 5% Muslim men commits nearly 77% of overall crimes inside Sweden, as per some reports between 2011 and 2014 Muslim men were found to be responsible to have raped more than 1000 Swedish women, a crime investigation report discovered that nearly 300 of those young girls raped are/were 15 years or less in age.

"Love Jihad" as it is called in India, call it Love-Jihad or Romeo-Jihad, apparently in India it is alleged by some right wing Hindu groups expressing their fear that the Sunni-Muslim cleric and priest largely encourages the young Sunni-Muslim boys to lure the Christian and Hindu girls and to indulge romantically and seduce them, once the romance reaches point of no return that's when Muslim boys systematically apply condition and forces the girls to convert to Islam so that they can get married, this is a ploy to increase their religion's numerical strength by converting girls to Islam.

Rape and seduce the girls, tarnish the dignity of the woman to such an extent, create compelling situation for woman to make compelling choice of marrying the ungracious Muslim man, so that the crafty man can further exploit the beleaguered woman.

CHILD brides as young as 12 have been ordered to stay with the men they were forced to marry after European officials agreed to recognize the partnerships. It comes amid fears of a Paedophilia epidemic inside European refugee camps after a pregnant 14-year-old girl went missing from a Dutch centre. The Netherlands is facing an issue of providing asylum to young girls who are married in their homeland but are below the Dutch age of consent. The number of underage girls, some as young as 11, being married to older men has tripled since the start of the war in Islamic countries, Poverty-stricken parents reluctantly agree to it when their savings run out and they can no longer afford to support their daughters. Now a generation of war babies are being born to mums who are still children themselves. A girl aged 11 or 12 marrying a man decades older than her is not a taboo but an accepted practice in Muslim society.

"Soeren Kern published an article about child sex slavery in the UK. He focuses on a report about the large-scale "grooming" of non-Muslim girls age between 11&16 by gangs of Muslim men into sex slavery. These men do not prey upon Muslim girls. The government, police force, and media have been "multi-culturally correct" and very reluctant to expose this phenomenon or to charge these men. Many feminists would say that men all over the world buy and sell women, kidnap or trick them into prostitution. And they are right. But they are wrong to refuse to focus on Paedophelia Sex Slavery wherever and whenever this monster rears its ugly head. The prepared report is meticulous. It documents that "officials in England and Wales were aware of rampant child grooming—the process by which sexual predators befriend and build trust with children in order to prepare them for abuse—by Muslim gangs since at least 1988."

Imagine that. Imagine being a young girl abused and the very people you are told will help you close their doors on you and worse still blames you for the abuse! The young women concerned are often seen by the Police as being deviant or promiscuous. The adult men with whom they are seen with are not questioned.

These accounts give us a harrowing perspective of the scale of the problem. How do we safeguard young vulnerable girls from those who want to exploit them? How do we inform the public to recognise a child who is being groomed? What use is all of this if the authorities are not going to help bring perpetrators to justice?

Women captives are sometimes forced to marry their Muslim masters, regardless of the marital status of the women. That is, the masters are allowed to have sex with the enslaved human property. It is one thing for some soldiers in any army to strike out on their own and rape women. All armies have criminal soldiers who commit this wrong act. But it is quite another to codify rape in a sacred text. Islam codifies and legalizes rape. It is disappointing that the Quran does not abolish this sexual crime in the clearest terms: Thou shalt not have sex with slave-girls under any circumstance!

According to news article published in "**Mail-online**" reported; "Migrants are being taught about gay sex, how to make love while pregnant and how to find the female G-spot in illustrated manuals distributed in Germany. Refugees in Germany are being taught about how to find the female G-spot, sex during pregnancy and how to enjoy homosexual sex.

The bizarre project – complete with graphic illustrations – is being financed by the German government.

In 13 languages on the government website **Zanzu**, all aspects of sexuality – from how to enjoy 'the first time' and how to avoid venereal diseases are tackled. Refugees in Germany are being taught about how to find the female G-spot, sex during pregnancy and how to enjoy homosexual sex on a website funded by the government. Topics include sex, virginity, the body and sex, the first time, sexual pleasure, sex during pregnancy and sexual problems and fears. It comes at a time when tensions between migrants and natives are still tense following the mass sexual assaults on women in Cologne on New Year's Eve.

The government said the guide was necessary because many of the 1.1 million refugees who have arrived in Germany since last year (2015) received no sexual education whatsoever in their homelands. And because many hold what are considered 'backward' views towards homosexuals – including attacking them in asylum centres – Berlin decided to issue the charts.

Refugees who have not been in the country long 'will receive discreet and direct access to knowledge in this area', said Elke Ferner, parliamentary state secretary in the ministry for family affairs.

As well as being available online and in some accommodation centres, many doctors and clinics charged with the health of migrants will receive the charts to better inform migrants about sex.

The Alternative for Germany (AfD) party which is riding high, declared the project 'a waste of taxpayer money.'"…

They (Germans) wonder whether the integration policy will be effective in folding potentially millions of refugees, from Syria to Eritrea, into conservative German society. No one wants a repeat of the "guest worker" era of the 1960s and 1970s, when one million or so foreigners, most of them from Turkey, were officially encouraged not to integrate; they formed their own communities on the fringes of German society, where many of them remain today. And liberal Germans wonder whether their country will lose its famously tolerant and open attitude towards outsiders. "Germany was already divided on taking refugees and now they will continue to be divided," "The [Cologne] incident (on "31st dec-2015" when it is alleged migrant Muslim men sexually abused and robbed German girls) is being used by the right wing to start a racist debate." Indeed, those on the far right, like the ultra-xenophobic party known as Pegida — Patriotic Europeans Against the

Islamization of the West – hijacked Cologne to pump up the volume of their anti-immigrant war cry.

"German chancellor Miss Angela Merkel" a highly regarded and rated as best politician and most powerful personality not only in Europe but in the world, Ms Merkel remarkably popular public figure and politician between 2010 and 2014, but her popularity took a severe beating and started to dwindle for her alleged softness towards Muslim community and her welcoming migrants and allowing refuge and asylum to those mostly Muslims migrating in to Europe from violence hit and war ravaged, poverty stricken Arabian and African Muslim dominated countries, incumbent German chancellor Merkel's open door refugee policy irked not only Germans but most Europeans as well, once most popular and powerful woman Angela Merkel towards the end of year 2015 became highly unpopular for her allege affection and sympathy for Islam and for helping migrating Muslims. Good times never remains good forever, Angela Merkel was severely criticized not only by German and European people but even politicians of many European countries and also from U.S.A vehemently criticized her for her role in dealing with refugee crisis, many people in Europe says it was Angela Merkel who was sending an open invitation to the refugees, Merkel's open invitation message **"Welcome to Germany" we'll help you all, we have a house and job for you in Germany, it is a good place to be in,"** encouraged many beleaguered people from war-ravaged Islamic countries to board and sail toward Europe and headed towards affluent European countries like Germany, Sweden, Austria and Norway etc.

Somewhat similar situation prevailed on other side of Atlantic ocean, like Germany's chancellor Angela Merkel another high profile and world famous woman politician U.S.A.'s **Miss Hillary Clinton** as well is or was accused in America for having a soft corner for Muslims and talking favorably for Islamic causes, both world's leading women politicians Germany's Angela Merkel and U.S.A.'s Hillary Clinton are or were brutally criticized for being more accommodative and helping Islamic causes. The rightist leaning and ultra conservative people in America and Europe are disgusted and dislikes their politicians paying steep refugee bills, taxpayer money being spent on paying hefty bills for cost incurred in providing Food, healthcare, housing, training etc, etc to millions of refugees and illegal immigrants pouring into Europe, that's, what irks the Americans and Europeans

Those migrants who've entered Europe from Muslim dominated Asian and African countries and most of them have succeeded in seeking refuge and asylum in Europe's most prosperous country Germany, for all their antics and misbehavior in open society, in many German cities you'll apparently see banners with slogans and comments written on the walls "**Rapefugees Not Welcome**," in 2016 more Germans who were initially silent have started voicing their concerns and turned against migrants and joined anti-Islam forces, fearing the worse social and economic consequences it would have as a result of expansion of Islam in European society.

Denmark, Sweden, Germany and Norway are some of the European nations which have between 2012 & 2015 seen and experienced unprecedented sexual violence and sharp rise in crime-rate, increase cases of pickpocketing and shoplifting. Some horrific reports alleges that some migrant cruel men most probably from Somalia, Pakistan and Afghanistan have allegedly been found involved in some outrageous crimes, breaking into houses and raping women and sodomize young children and gatecrashing into public toilets and washrooms and forcefully indulged in shameless sexual activities. Not surprising Police authorities in many European countries have advised European girls and women also to gays and bio-sexual to take extra precautions and not to step out and walk alone on roads and streets at nights.

From women's perspective, a woman's most valuable asset is her **Vagina**, but when this precious asset is torn apart by a voracious man, when a man to soothe his mind and for fulfilment of his desire of indulging in sexual fantasy forcefully sucks in his Peni into woman's vagina, what a horrible incident that proves to be for that hapless woman who suffers such excruciating pain, one can only imagine.

A woman who gets raped, have to, for rest her of the life live with taboo and stigma. The effects are deep and long lasting.

This post-traumatic stress can manifest itself in nightmares or flashbacks, where the woman feels she is once again experiencing the attack. "She can smell the alcohol on the breath of the rapist and it doesn't feel as if it is happening years ago.

It has become common place for Muslims to make demands upon others to adhere to their standards. So obscene and common decency are opposing elements, which exist precisely because of their opposition. The shame, feelings of shame, embarrassment, repulsion is typical of the individual when he, against his will, finds himself in front of other people's events do not correspond to their education and culture, and reputed for its scandalous sex education.

Modesty becomes common sense when human society membership shares the same sensitivity towards the female body which in some Eastern societies if not fully covered may be considered obscene. The reference culture manages the lives of their bodies and every aspect and functionality, the speech also closely linked to sexuality.

....

The sad truth is that the dominant Western policy towards the Arab people traditionally has been one of containment. Today many applaud as the people of the region take to the streets to claim their rights, but until recently Western governments frequently acted as if the Arab people were to be feared, hemmed in controlled. The Arab Spring showed that many people in the region do not share the West's comfortable complacency with autocratic rule. No longer willing to be the passive subjects of self-serving rulers, they began to insist on becoming full citizens of their countries, the proper agents of their fate.

Article title; **Avoid a classic blunder: stay out of religion wars in the Middle East**: "Muslims in the Middle East are fighting wars of religion. Like the carnage between Protestants and Catholics that haunted Northern Ireland during the last third of the 20th century, there is little anyone can do until local peoples crave peace so intensely they are willing to cultivate it. History shows that outside meddling only intensifies sectarian fury. Stopping internecine war begins at home. President Barack Obama imperils Americans by trying to excise an abscess that can be cured only from the inside out. The decision to re-engage in Iraq, and the wider Middle East, also contradicts the president's other, bigger objective: to exit the nanny business. The last time religious aggression swept an entire subcontinent was during the Reformation four centuries ago, when Christians hashed out their hatreds much as Muslims of the Middle East are doing today. Islamic State (ISIS), or as the President Obama calls it, the Islamic State in Iraq and the Levant, is fighting to restore a caliphate. Catholics and Protestants spent decades warring over similar issues. Should all Christians accept the same religious doctrine? Should all nations be under the dominion of the pope?

The first Islamic Civil War, from 656 to 661, created two competitive sects – Sunni and Shi'ite. Neither recognized the other's legitimacy.

Sunnis bowed to a caliph who ruled over all believers regardless of nationality. The last caliph was Sultan Abdülmecid II. Kemal Ataturk, the resolute builder of modern Turkey, fired Abdülmecid in 1924. The 400-year-old caliphate in Istanbul vanished. Unsurprisingly, not everyone was happy about the rupture. In 1928, the Muslim Brotherhood began in Egypt. That group and other like-minded sectarian organizations gradually spread into the new secular nations of Syria, Jordan, Iraq and Iran." ------Elizabeth Cobbs Hoffman,"--------

The Sunni-Muslim men do not value women they do not understand the pain of the women, how much a women suffers, Muslim men without any regrets remorselessly rapes and sexually exploits non-Muslim women, particularly young girls and women from Hindu and Christian communities. Islamists set their own agenda, even if living and earning livelihood in non-Islamic country Muslims do not respect **national anthem** of that country, Muslims disrespect <u>flags and national anthems</u> of non-Muslim countries similarly like Sunni Muslims disrespect women of non-Muslim communities, Muslim folks have serious mental problems, Muslims living in non-Islamic countries wants marriage laws and divorce procedures as per sharia, Islamists have problems with conventional banking system they insist on Islamic style banking in which lending institutions are barred from investing or lending money to tobacco and alcohol companies. Muslims defies conventional norms, be it in fashion industry as well, instead of wearing more conventional form of swimwear, Muslim women instead of wearing traditional two piece **Bikini**, they wear fully covered **Burkini** and takes plunge in swimming pool, Muslim men as well can be seen swimming wearing Pyjama or full pants. Such abnormal behavior of Muslims is the reason why Muslims are becoming more and more isolated, and therefore it is becoming "**Islam versus the rest – third world war**," Muslims do not want to integrate with other communities and do not want to adopt modern norms and way of life.

On the larger geopolitical level, meanwhile, one thing appears to be certain: the west will have less impact in shaping the Arab world's future than in decades past. The reasons for this are varied: they include the more complex internal politics of western states, which have been badly affected both by the economic and financial crisis since 2008 and by the costly, inconclusive wars in Afghanistan and Iraq. These factors have resulted in greater caution about foreign-policy entanglements, and this in turn reinforces ongoing changes in the geo-economic balance of power worldwide. In this fluid situation, neither regional powers nor global institutions appear ready on their own to fill gaps in authority or provide new direction.

Decades after emancipation from colonial rule, the quest for independence still figures highly on the Arab agenda, and in this quest the pursuit of authenticity has moved to centre stage. Authenticity represents, of course, a highly complex concept, more complex at any rate than many of its partisans would have their audiences believe. While some debate the relative weight of Arabism versus local attachments (Egyptian identity, Iraqi nationalism), Islamist activists have a simple answer: Authenticity is identical with Islam -- not the Islam actually practiced by the so-called popular masses, an Islam already corrupted by misconceptions, magic and superstition, but the true Islam of the age of the Prophet and his Companions, or rather their image of that true Islam. This Islam, so they claim, is the solution to all problems of private and public life, of state and society, the yardstick by which to measure values, goals and institutions. Western techniques and modes of organization may be acceptable, but there is a strict refusal to adopt un-Islamic values. The distinction at once complicates the matter, for liberal democracy clearly involves both techniques and values.

It is this. If Christian churches throughout U.S.A. trained their flocks in political action, advocated a foreign, fascist political system, preached hatred towards other religions, and sent funds to foreign movements to support anti-American activities, they would most certainly lose their tax exempt status. They would no longer be classified as "houses of worship" but would be classified as houses of political action - actually seditious political action. That is exactly what is being taught and promoted in Islamic mosques and "training centers" throughout U.S., CAIR is being exposed for their seditious actions. In the U.S, Muslims most often work to "influence", or in Christian terms, "evangelize". In political terms, they are lobbyists for their cause. In commercial terms, they are promoters of their cause. Of course, there is the occasional "sudden Jihadi syndrome" that erupts in violent acts such as at Fort Hood. Or intricately planned attacks such as 9-11. In countries with greater concentrations of Muslims, they are more aggressive, practicing more overt forms of coercion often through fairly frequent acts of terror. And in Islamic nations that are threatened with western intervention, terror acts are daily occurrences.

In 2010 Muslims made up 11.7% of the population in Russia, according to rough estimate as of 2014 it has risen to 14%, various statistics proves that when Muslim population hits 5% in any country, that country begins to experience major social problems and violence. "Muslim militants kill the men but take the women to have sex with them. And then after they have used them for a number of months, they're so distraught mentally and physically that then they may let them go or they may kill them (beleaguered women)."

In 15th century came the formation of Muslim Crimean Khanate which occupied the Black Sea shores and the southern steppes of Ukraine. Until the late 18th century, Ottoman forces under "Gedik Ahmed Pasha" conquered all of the Crimean peninsula and joined it to the khanate in 1475. During the 16th and 17th centuries, it was an important centre of the slave trade, the Crimean Khanate maintained an enormous slave trade with the Ottoman Empire and the Middle-east between 1500 and 1700A.D in which Muslim merchants exported over 2 million slaves from Russia and Ukraine. Native Russians and Ukrainians, because of their fair skin were in huge demand as slaves (mainly women). Hence targeted for kidnapping and slavery. The Crimean Khanate was a Turkic vassal state of Ottoman Empire during 1478 to 1774, later it was dissolved by Russian empire in 1783. The Crimean Khanate was one of the many remnants of the Golden Horde, the north-western division of the separated Mongol Empire. Located north of the Black Sea, the Crimean Khanate also proved to be the most lasting remnant. The term "Tatar" derives from an old Mongolian tribe. It eventually came to be a term used by Europeans for the inhabitants and warriors of Mongol Empire as a whole, especially the Golden Horde division. The majority of Ukrainian Muslims are from Crimean Tatar background. Because of violent nature of Islam and the kidnappings and forced slavery mostly of women, Islam was repressed in Russia starting from Russian conquest of Kazan in 1552 until the rise of Catherine the great in 1762.

There have been large-scale atrocities on the Continent in recent years—in Madrid, London, and at the Charlie Hebdo offices, in Paris, in January of year 2015—but in the aftermath of this one there is a realization that Europe, its cities, and all those institutions predicated on unending peace are now vulnerable to bewilderingly rapid developments. Turkey is reluctant to readmit large numbers of migrants - but it is under intense EU pressure now to do so. Under the current rules, only migrants who have no right to international protection can be sent back to Turkey. That means economic migrants. The reason is that only one EU country considers Turkey "safe" for returning migrants. EU data shows that 23% of asylum claims from migrants of Turkish origin were deemed well-founded in 2014. Turkey is demanding a high price for its co-operation, arguing that it has already spent €8bn helping refugees from the Syrian war. It is struggling with the influx, already housing 2.5 million in camps. As a candidate to join the EU, Turkey wants to see real progress in its accession negotiations. The EU has pledged that, and is offering visa-free travel for Turkish citizens in the Schengen passport-free zone. Historic tension between Greece and Turkey makes the Aegean operation to stem the migrant flow difficult - as does Turkey's long, zig-zagging coastline. Europe is beset by so many crisis that it can be hard to remember them all. In rough order of prominence, they are: home-grown terrorism, the largest migration of people since World War II, sovereign debt, doubts about the euro's viability, the rise of extreme right-wing parties such as France's National Front, Russia's menace to its western neighbours, growing Euro-Scepticism.

The migrants who embark upon this journey are typically represented as terrorized and impoverished—as people driven (to quote Amnesty International) "to risk their lives in treacherous sea crossings in a desperate attempt to reach safety in Europe." The demographic and economic facts complicate that story. When populations flee war or famine, they generally flee together: the elderly and the infants, women as well as men. The current migrants, however, are overwhelmingly working-age males. All of them have paid a substantial price to make the trip: it can cost upwards of $2,000 to board a smuggler's boat, to say nothing of hundreds or even thousands of dollars to travel from home to the embarkation point in the first place. Very few of the migrants from Libya are actually Libyan nationals.

Article title "The refugee crisis: why we need to speak about corruption," have reported: "Although corruption alone is not a direct reason why refugees flee their countries, **research** shows it is often a chief contributor to the overall violence and instability forcing people to run for their physical and psychological safety. Widespread corruption undermines the legitimacy and stability of a government especially if it fails to meet the needs of its people. Research also shows that corruption prolongs armed conflict and violence and weakens peace-building efforts. Corruption facilitates cross-border smuggling of weapons and insurgents as well as the flow of monies from contraband activities that fuels wars. The trafficking of human beings as well as refugee smuggling, which has become a multi-billion dollar business, thrives on corruption. Bribery occurs at almost every stage of people smuggling from the start to the final destination.

Smugglers often bribe national and foreign officials to issue fraudulent passports and visas as well as border control and immigration officers to turn a blind eye to refugees as they pass. The lack of safe passage for refugees have forced them to pay as high as **US$3,000** per person to reach Europe. Such corrupt and criminal smuggling rings give refugees the opposite of what they seek, safety. Dodgy **rubber** dinghies, **fake** life vests, or captains who **abandon** their ships, have led to thousands of refugees tragically dying in the Mediterranean Sea en-route to Europe.".........

Along the Balkan migrant route, an undetermined number of men, women and children considered economic migrants have found themselves stranded, their hopes of reaching prosperous northern EU countries dashed by border closures. Greece, with thousands of miles of coastline, is the only country that cannot feasibly block people from entering without breaking international laws about rescuing those in distress at sea. Europe's response to the crisis has been fractured, with individual countries, concerned about the sheer scale of the influx, introducing new border controls aimed at limiting the flow. The problem is compounded by the reluctance of many migrants' countries of origin, such as Pakistan, to accept forcible returns.

Many politicians and also media journalists in U.S.A. and Europe have ever since the start of refugee and migration crisis have been voicing concern and also taunting the wealthy oil rich Arab countries of not doing enough or rather doing nothing to help people fleeing from war torn Islamic countries, accusation especially targeted towards Saudi Arabia the same country which is also birth place of Islam, reminding them of their holy-duty of being more accommodative and so to render asylum and refuge to at least those Sunni folks who are escaping brutality and fleeing from war torn, violence hit and poverty stricken nations like Iraq, Afghanistan, Syria, Libya and also Pakistan, requesting Saudis, Qataris and Kuwaitis to allow entry to migrants in the kingdom (Saudi Arabia) and also in Qatar.

It won't be fair to accuse the Saudis, Qataris or Kuwaiti governments, it is not as if the Saudi government had closed its doors and did not allowed entry to the migrants who are/were running away from violence and wars and also fed-up of poverty and social problems in their own Islamic country. It is so that the last thing a Muslim from Iraq, Syria, Afghanistan, Pakistan or any such country want to do is to seek asylum or refuge in a Islamic country like Saudi Arabia, whether it is deliberate as part of their long term strategy to populate non-Islamic countries or it is unintentional, this is highly debatable subject matter. But Muslims for whatever reasons best known to them they always prefer to migrate and settle in non-Muslim ruled country, therefore their preferred choice is Europe, north-America or Australia anywhere but Islamic countries.

Are Muslims especially the Sunni-Muslims deliberately populating non-Islamic countries to achieve something bigger for their religion in long term? Is the **Islamic army** strategically working on a game plan to take full control of global economics and politics? These questions have meaning but is highly controversial subject matter, controversial topic to debate. But at least one thing the Islamists have categorically made clear they'll destroy everything that is un-Islamic in this world.

But then, as we observe there is so much fighting in Islamic countries itself. Why Islamists can't find solutions for Islamic problems? Islamic wars and problems are as complex as much complex is the conflict in Muslim dominated countries. The reasons for savage differences over religious issues and violence varies from country to country, different Islamic or Muslim dominated countries have different and differing problems. To have better perspective of Islamic problems and reason for wars in Muslim dominated countries; Like for example in countries such as Iraq, Syria and Yemen, it is war for supremacy between two main rival faction of Islam the Shiites and Sunnis, in these countries both the Shia army led by Iranians and Sunni jihadists allegedly aided and supported by Saudis and Qataris are battling out in open battlefields.

While other Islamic countries like Somalia and Libya it is a chaotic situation, complete breakdown of governing system, economic and political system have totally collapsed in these two Muslim country.

In Saudi Arabia majority Sunni population is supressing and humiliating minority Shia community, apart from sectarian rift in Saudi there are many other thorny issues, Cultural, philosophical and religious issues, following and governing kingdom based on Hardline harsh Islamic religious law, discriminating local Saudi citizens because there is no freedom of speech and expression, beheading those who dares to speak against or commit any sort of crime and those unfortunate individuals who are found guilty of having violated Islamic principles, according to reports each year at least 600 people are beheaded in Saudi Arabia.

Egypt known as land of Pharaohs, an Islamic country now, the problem in Egypt is cultural and ideological, country is bitterly divided on cultural lines, a tussle between Moderates, liberals and radicals, liberal thinking Egyptians are in favour of more freedom and secular values, on the other side are forces who wants Egypt to have Islamic religious law and lifestyle as permitted by Islam, so it is more of a cultural problem in Egypt, liberals and secular forces defending themselves from extremist Islamic army.

While Turkey another critically important nation for both Islam and for the western countries, here the problems are different from other Islamic countries. Turkey predominately a Sunni Muslim country, the Sunni Arabs and Turks have serious fundamental "Political, cultural and economic" differences and problems with powerful regional ethnic **Kurdish** community, in Turkey the fight is between Sunni security forces and Kurdish liberation army.

Likewise there are internal rift and brutal differences in many other Islamic nations, no matter whatever differences and troubles are there among Muslims, yet, the Sunni faction of Islam is united in their resolve to establish <u>Sunni- Islam caliphate</u> all over the world.

It is all on record, evidently Islam have increased influence and gain maximum possible control over Africa, many African countries which were once ruled by Christians or Pagans, are now under control of Islam, if we take into account atrocities committed by Islamic forces and militants in Africa, between 1980 and 2015 Islamist militants have terrorize entire north & central African region and also not spared east-Africa, Sunni Islamic army have caused maximum possible damage and destruction to properties and lives of Christians and few surviving Pagan religious communities, rampant killings and massacres and forceful conversions, Christians and Pagans were forced to convert to Islam, those who refused to embrace Islam were mercilessly killed.

"Article **"The Islamic Effect on Africa"** describes; "Only the narrow stretch of the Red Sea separates the Arabian peninsula from North Africa, and Islam reached Africa quickly after the birth of Islam in A.D. 610. Consequently, Egypt was the first country to come under Islamic influence and provided the Arabs with an important gateway into the rest of Africa. The Arab traders were accomplished seafarers who were able to cross this route and the Indian Ocean. They also used the Nile River to take them south. In addition, the prospect of crossing the Sahara Desert to head west did not faze these desert dwellers.

One of the primary effects of the spread of Islam into North Africa was the acceptance of the Arabic language. Language is one of the main cultural influences left behind by most invading forces: the Romans brought Latin to its European conquests, providing the roots of modern Romance languages and much of

English, and through political control, the Arabs made Arabic the predominant language in North Africa. There is no other part of Africa where political control went hand in hand with the spread of Islam. Islamic expansion into Morocco also paved the way for the invasion of southern Spain that introduced Islam into Europe."......

As of September-2015, Muslim population world over was 1.65 Billion. Of which Sunni faction of Islam dominating with approximate 1.18 Billion, remaining approximately 350 or 360 Million belonging to Shiite faction of Islam.

Islam is fast expanding its bases and numerical strength in Europe, not only in Europe, worldwide Islam is fastest growing religion, every other non-Islamic religions, have a very tepid growth rate, a rough estimate indicates that all other major religions such as "Christianity, Hinduism or Buddhism" are growing at dismal 0.80% to 1.70% annually, in stark contrast Muslims have higher birth rate therefore world's Muslim population is growing at 4% to 5% annually, so if Muslim folks maintains same population growth rate for few more decades, than a most conservative estimate suggest by year 2050 Muslim population in world is most likely to cross **3 Billion**. So such a spectacular population growth rate of Muslims, do other communities needs to be concern about Muslim population crossing 3 Billion Mark? Again a tough one, a simple question, yet difficult to answer it, time alone will tell.

Islam's problems are complex, when Islam is in trouble, it causes pain and creates problems for the entire world's population. However fast growing Muslim population has helped Islamists gradually gain control of some of the most strategically situated countries in the world. While countries in southern parts of African continent have less Muslim population hence have less Islamic influence, therefore southern African countries are ruled and governed by either Christians or indigenous African religious communities leaders, but story is lot different in rest of Africa, entire Northern, central, western regions of African continent have large Muslim population hence many countries in northern, central and western Africa are ruled by Muslims. Similarly like Africa, most parts of large Asian continent have super-large Muslim population, apart from west-Asia majority of countries in central Asia as well in south-Asia are overwhelmingly dominated by Muslims, in east-Asia as well apart from Indonesia and Malaysia many other countries as well have large Muslim population. So as it is evident that two of the continent Asia and

Africa are firmly in grip of Islam, and if current trend persists in Europe, unless something dramatic happens otherwise by year 2070 Islam will be majority religion in Europe, hence many European countries will have Muslim Prime-minister or President, therefore don't be surprise, it is likely that by (year) 2075 many European countries will be ruled and governed by Islamic forces.

Numbers game, politics is all about numbers, any particular ethnic or religious community which has numbers or to say have higher population in any particular country, in which case it is all obvious that particular ethnic or religious community will control and dominate that particular country's economic and political system.

In one of the article **"Islam is on the rise in Europe - The Islamic bulletin"** narrated; "Islam is the second largest religion in Europe today. In spite of periodic persecution and discrimination, Islam seems to be not only surviving but steadily growing in numbers of converts and influence. With the Serbian aggression against Bosnia-Herzegovina, a Muslim country, interest by people is growing in learning about Islam and Muslims.

The Muslims in Western Europe are those who emigrated from Africa, the Middle East and the Indo-Pakistan subcontinent after the Second World War.

Due to manpower shortages and industrial growth in Western Europe after the Second World War, substantial numbers of Muslims migrated to Western Europe. These Muslims kept their cultural, religious and ethnic links with their mother countries.

Today these Muslims and their descendants, along with a growing number of native people who are accepting Islam have made the Muslim population the second largest in many parts of Europe.

Austria, Belgium, Britain, Denmark, France, Italy, Holland, Sweden, Spain, Switzerland, and Germany have large Muslim populations which are growing every day. The Muslim community of these countries need separate articles to cover their growing social, cultural, and economic role in Western Europe.

Reliable figures on the Muslim population in Western Europe are not available. However, it is believed that an estimated 10 million Muslims live in Western

Europe today. France, Germany, and Britain have the largest Muslim populations. Muslim sources estimate that both France and Germany have about three million Muslims each, while Britain is said to have about two million. As in Britain, Islam has been the second largest religion in France since the 1970's. By the year 2,000, Muslims are expected to make up more than 10 percent of the French population.

By the mid 1980's, there was no Western European government that had not instituted some legal measures to stop further immigration of Muslim people from Asia, Africa and other parts of the world.

Large numbers of Europeans have converted to Islam in the last two decades. Their actual number remains unknown. The majority of these conversions have been made through the efforts of different ways or Islamic Sufi brotherhood and the Darqawiyahs which claim a link with the Arab-Moroccan city of Fez. Most of the Darqawi converts are drawn from the solid professional middle class and seek a return to the early traditions of Islam. European converts to Islam have included a number of prominent figures, especially in the academic life. This group includes Baron Omar Ehrenfels, the Austrian anthropologist (d. 1930); Vincent Morteil, the specialist on African and Islamic affairs, Michel Chodkiewicz, director of the French publishing house Editions du Seuil; and Roger Garudy, the French philosopher and former communist party member.

Several countries in Western Europe have recognized the Muslim feasts and holidays. Broadcast time has also been allowed to Muslims in France and some other countries. But problems remain. Muslims and Islam are still treated unfairly in the media. Any attempt by a Muslim society to make Islam as its foundation of life is seen as a challenge to western civilization and is immediately labeled as fundamentalist or terrorist.".........

"More recent study and data suggests that **as of 2014** Muslim population in **Europe**, there are approximately 6.5 million Muslims living in Germany, and in France have Muslim population of 6 million, while U.K., and Italy have roughly 3 million each, but maximum Muslim population is in Russia estimated to be about 16.5 million."

During the reigns of the first four caliphs (632-661), Islam spread rapidly. The wars of expansion were also advanced by the devotion of the faithful to the concept of jihad. Muslims are obliged to extend the faith to

unbelievers and to defend Islam from attack. The original concept of jihad did not include aggressive warfare against non-Muslims, but "holy war" was sometimes waged by Muslims whose interpretation of the Koran allowed them such
latitude. Jihad was directly responsible for some of the early conquests of Islam outside of the Arabian Peninsula.

Expansion of Islam in Europe and north-America, what will be medium and long term social effects? How expansion of Islam in Europe will alter political equations? **They are Migrants or Islamic Army**! The European countries are becoming increasingly unsafe, as it is, Europe has been experiencing exponential increase in crimes and criminal activities, between years 2004 and 2014 crimes in Europe has considerably risen higher, and most of the perpetrated crimes are committed by the immigrants and not surprisingly among the immigrants it is the Muslims who are involve in most of the crime cases, so recorded Crime-Data proves Muslims are perpetrating maximum crimes in Europe.

For Europeans other cause of concern also is very high percentage of youth unemployment, according to some estimates at the end of the calendar year 2014 as much as 30% of young men and women in age group of 18 to 34 were/are either unemployed or underemployed, adding to the woes of the European countries is the inrush of immigrants from Africa and West-Asian Islamic countries, the times ahead, in years and decades to come could be full of anguish and turbulence for the Europeans.

Not much happening, economic growth in Europe is subdued, no major business investments in industrial projects, falling fertility rates, European women preferring to delay marriage and pregnancy, chronic demographic problems in Europe, in contrast the Muslims are profound proliferators, the birth rate and population growth of Muslim community is highest in the world, Muslim community is largely socially conservative, average Muslim girls get married at early age, so you'll find many Muslim women who by the time they celebrate their 25th birthday they are already mother of 3 or 4 children. Fundamental ground realities is what is concerning many in Europe, and European community is divided, while the moderates and liberal thinking Europeans are willing and favouring giving shelter to those hard pressed migrant refugees entering European shore to seek refuge, another section of rightist leaning and conservative Europeans are opposing tooth and nail any move of their respective country government and politicians to provide refuge to migrant refugees, also keeping in mind the fact that many of those who are seeking refuge in several prosperous European countries are conservative Sunni Muslims, the reason why significantly large section of Europeans are jittery and apprehensive is because they seriously fear that once the Islamic folks establishes themselves and strengthen their bases inside continental Europe they will destroy millennium old European civilizations, will profoundly harm European culture and traditions and destroy ancient artistic structures, fears emanates from the fact that Muslims have smashed and destroyed traditional art and culture in many African and Asian countries.

The European society will become brutally polarize on Racial, Religious and linguistic lines, with growing immigrant population and maximum number of those immigrants belonging to the Muslim community. The difference over culture and religion will only grow between the Neo-Nazis and the Muslims in Europe, the European rightist leaning right-wing extremists groups and Muslim community intensely dislike each other, which apparently will potentially increase hatred crimes on streets of various European cities because local citizens will become more intolerant and impatient. Because of lower business investments there are too few jobs available hence lot more people will have to compete for the same available few jobs. With rising unemployment and so much uncertainty in Europe, it is likely that situation will implode and get chaotic totally out of control and Europe would potentially become one of the world's most unstable region and plunge into full blown social and economic crisis, fears of urban guerrilla warfare fought in principle European town and cities looms large, which will be catastrophic and social tension will be many – many times severe and brutal than it was experienced in the 1920s and 1940s. If religious intolerance between Muslims and Non-Muslim communities rises and extremism accelerates, it will potentially create Political instability and law and order problems across Europe, Europe could once again formally become an Axis centre for the official start of "**WW 3**.

How Islam spread in Europe? "**Wikipedia --- Islam in Europe**" writes; "Muslim forays into Europe began shortly after the religion's inception, with a short lived invasion of Byzantine Sicily by a small Arab and Berber force that landed in 652. Islam gained its first genuine foothold in continental Europe from 711 onward, with the Umayyad conquest of Hispania. The invaders named their land Al-Andalus, which expanded to include what is now Portugal and Spain except for the northern highlands of Asturias, Basque country, Navarra and few other places protected by mountain chains from southward invasions.

Al-Andalus has been estimated to have had a Muslim majority by the 10th century after most of the local population converted to Islam.[6]:42 This coincided with the *La Convivencia* period of the Iberian Peninsula as well as the **Golden age of Jewish culture in Spain**. Pelayo of Asturias began the Christian counter-offensive known as the Reconquista after the Battle of Covadonga in 722. Slowly, the Christian forces began a conquest of the fractured taifa kingdoms of al-Andalus. By 1236, practically all that remained of Muslim Spain was the southern province of Granada.".........

Historically the relations have never been cordial between Islam and Europeans, there has always been distrust and hatred and many wars, many times the two opposing armies have confronted each other in battlefield **"Wikipedia "Balkan wars"** has written; "The Ottoman Empire lost all its European territories to the west of the River **Maritsa** as a result of the two Balkan Wars, which thus delineated present-day Turkey's western border. A large influx of Turks started to flee into the Ottoman heartland from the lost lands. By 1914, the remaining core region of the Ottoman Empire had experienced a population increase of around 2.5 million because of the flood of immigration from the Balkans.

Citizens of Turkey regard the Balkan Wars as a major disaster (*Balkan harbi faciası*) in the nation's history. The unexpected fall and sudden relinquishing of Turkish-dominated European territories created a **psycho-traumatic** event amongst the Turks that is said to have triggered the ultimate **collapse** of the empire itself within five years. **Nazım Pasha**, Chief of Staff of the Ottoman army, was held responsible for the failure and was assassinated on 23 January 1913 during the 1913 Ottoman coup d'état carried out by the "Young Turks."

The **First Balkan War** broke out when the League member states attacked the Ottoman Empire on 8 October 1912 and ended seven months later with the signing of the **Treaty of London** on 30 May 1913. The Second Balkan War broke out on 16 June 1913. Both Serbia and Greece, utilizing the argument that the war had been prolonged, repudiated important particulars of the pre-war treaty and retained occupation of all the conquered districts in their possession which were to be divided according to specific predefined boundaries. Seeing the treaty as trampled, <u>Bulgaria</u> was dissatisfied over the division of the spoils in <u>Macedonia</u> (made in secret by its former allies, Serbia and Greece) and commenced military action against them. The more numerous combined Serbian and Greek armies repelled the Bulgarian offensive and counter-attacked into <u>Bulgaria</u>. <u>Romania</u>, who having taken no part in the conflict, had intact armies to strike with, invaded Bulgaria from the north in violation of a peace treaty between the two states. The Ottoman Empire also attacked <u>Bulgaria</u> and advanced in Thrace regaining <u>Adrianople.</u> In the resulting <u>Treaty of Bucharest</u>, Bulgaria lost most of the territories it had gained in the First Balkan War in addition to being forced to cede the ex-Ottoman south-third of <u>Dobroudja</u> province to <u>Romania</u>."…………

What we see is not a lack of solidarity; what we see is a clash of solidarities: national, ethnic and religious solidarity chafing against our obligations as human beings. But it's not just a matter of self-pity. Despite living at the crossroads of Europe and Asia, Russia and the Middle East, many Eastern Europeans are incurious and insular. Building a <u>Statue of Liberty</u> on Lampedusa will hardly be enough to deal with the problem. Libya and Syria are frustrating examples: Neither the European intervention in Libya nor its nonintervention in Syria have been able to stop the wars in Europe's neighborhood. Being poorer than Western Europeans, after the collapse of <u>Communism</u> in east Europe in 1990s and at the time of east-Europe's political and economic unification with west-European nations, now they (east-Europeans) point out, how can anyone expect solidarity from us? We were promised tourists, not refugees. Torn between its moral obligation to help others in extreme need and the practical impossibility of helping everybody.

It apparently is not as if only the Europeans have to worry about with regards to intelligence report that some among the migrant Muslims in disguise are well trained members of Islamic Jihadi army, but they also have to be concern about the home grown Jihadis, the radicalization process in Europe began much before the 2014/15 migrant crisis, Radical Islam has spread and is spreading across Europe among descendants of Muslim immigrants, *Disenfranchised and upset* by the failure of integration in mainstream European society, desperate times call for desperate measures, because immigrant Sunni Muslims felt rejected by the Europeans, many deeply committed European Islamists have adopted aggressive approach, hence many Muslims have taken up jihad (Islam holy war) against western countries and western civilization, these <u>Europe's Angry Muslims</u> or the jihadists are dangerous because they are committed to Islamic doctrine, not only European nations and ethnic Europeans have to fear and worry, but these jihadists Islamic armed forces can enter United States of America without visas. As it is the Islamic jihadi network is or has spread throughout Europe from Poland to Portugal all thanks to Islamic extremism or to say spread of radical Islam among the descendants guest workers once recruited by European industries to shore up Europe's post-war economic miracle. Whether it is in smoky coffeehouses in Rotterdam and Stockholm, or in makeshift Muslim prayer halls in Copenhagen and Brussels, or in Islamic religious bookstalls in Birmingham and London, or and in the prison cells in Madrid, Milan and Paris, immigrants or their descendants belonging to Sunni Muslim community are vehemently volunteering for jihad against western countries, Jihadi terrorists hitting hard at soft targets making Europeans and the Americans equally vulnerable.

A look in the mirror of the past may humble us, whether past history or present times Europeans have seen and experienced it all, in 20th century 2 devastatingly brutal World-Wars were fought which left Europe in smouldering ruins, **Holocaust** arguably the worse human tragedy in human history, disintegration of Yugoslavia and collapse of communist regimes in east-Europe in early 1990s and subsequent heart-wrenching ferocious Bosnian war and Balkan war between 1991 & 2001 in which tens of thousands people were killed and millions were displaced.

In 21st century; Among prominent European cities, <u>London</u> and Spanish city <u>Madrid</u> were the first to have experienced devastating terror attacks by Islamic jihadists, but again in November-2015 terror attacks in <u>Paris</u> in which more than 125 innocent civilians were killed, and few months later March-2016 massive terror attacks in Belgium capital city of Brussels. Brussels is not only capital of Belgium but home to European Union, all major institutions, commercial and administrative offices and European parliament is/are situated in Brussels, so to say that Brussels is nerve centre of Europe. So the Islamic terrorist groups in 21st century are or have been systematically targeting prominent European cities and strategic locations. It is not just killings but Islamic jihadi army motives it seem is to terrorize and traumatize the entire European population.

If we assess ground realities between 2008 and 2015, there's plenty of problems European have to deal with, stagnant and subdued economic growth, appalling job market, younger demographic particularly unable to find suitable jobs and economic opportunities. European economy feeling deflationary pressure, Europe's problem for long has been <u>not inflation</u> but **deflation**, prices of essential consumer products and items are not rising because people as well as businesses are not spending, people are spending less because people do not have more money in their pockets to spend lavishly. And further adding to already heavily encumbered Europeans with all sorts of social and economic problems are large inflow of people migrating from Arabian and African war-ravaged and poverty stricken Islamic countries.

Far too many problems for Europeans to tolerate.

First terror attacks in Paris later terror attacks in Brussels, many intellectuals and academicians started debating whether to disband EU (European union), as of 2015 approximately 28 big and small European countries have come together and formed EU (European union), EU is politics and economic union among 28 member states, some argue that longer than expected economic recession and slower economic growth, besides serious economic problems in member country <u>Greece</u>, and many other problems like rising crime rates, increase in Islamic terrorism, growing religious intolerance, Islamic jihadists openly challenging European authorities that they'll not rest until such time they takeover entire Europe and hoist **Islamic Flag** in Rome and Paris. This precisely is the reason many believe EU needs to be dissolve so that large European nations such as Germany, Italy and France can be free to evolve their own economic and monetary policies, have their own currency and each nation takes full responsibility of managing and securing their respective country's borders, also each country can draft and implement their own immigration policies.

Great Britain (United Kingdom) a very important country and dominant player in international politics, at the time of me writing this book, it is hotly being debated and discussed "whether U.K should remain part of EU (European union) or should Britain exit (Brexit) from EU." Fierce debate among British politicians and business lobby, many favour Britain staying united and strengthen its relation with EU, while those who are not in favour of Britain staying with EU they suggest and advice Breaking all existing ties with EU and have its (Britain) own complete independent Economic, politics & foreign policies, renegotiate trade and business pacts and re-work on foreign policies, those British nationals who were earlier undecided which way to vote and whom to favour, but after terror attacks first Paris and later in Brussels in March-2016, growing feeling of insecurity and anxiety among Britishers hence change in thinking, so more number of people believe their country will be better off alone, immediately after Brussels terror attacks many took it to the social media to voice their concern and some supposedly Britain's nationals were writing comments and posting blogs some of the message were **"We British love Europe and European people but not EU (European Union) we'll be better alone,"** so opinions change rapidly, in our life there is no stability, time changes very fast advantage turns into disadvantage and disadvantage turns into advantage all can potentially happen in matter of moments

Once in a year 1968 British politician **Enoch Powell** in his famous speech commonly called **"Rivers of Blood"** criticizing *Commonwealth immigration and anti-discrimination legislation* he had warned and had said, "allowing excess immigration, United Kingdom was "heaping up its own funeral pyre" bringing major religious and cultural changes in British society." Enoch Powell speech apparently caused political storm and damaged what otherwise at that time was a promising career.

The frequent brutal assaults by terrorist groups owing allegiance to Islam with great degree of consistency, targeting innocent civilian population and killing mainly Non-Muslims, is all but obvious to spark anti-Muslim backlash, as it said, that, for every action there is a reaction, and for every reaction there is a counter reaction, so not surprising for brutal inhuman activities of several Islamist terrorist organizations it was obvious to have a retaliatory reaction and inevitable retribution, I've observed and it has been reported in media as well that Islamophobia reached all time high during 2015, anti-Islam sentiments all over from Russia to Europe to America, non-Islamic communities infuriated with acts of Muslim jihadists, their anger began to be felt, hate crimes against Muslims started increasing especially in Europe and in U.S., because majority of innocent people killed by jihadists are/were Europeans and Americans.

It is indeed worrisome for those folks who love to live in peace, as abrupt rise in islamophobia will bring further pain to humanity, because the Far-Right and Right-wing politicians and political parties are trying to take advantage of prevailing anti-Islam sentiments, similar to what Adolf Hitler did when he made political capital in 1920s/30s by taking advantage of than prevailing Anti-Semitic and anti-Jewish sentiments in Europe particularly in Germany.

Similarly in 21st century, quick to take advantage of prevailing anti-Muslim sentiments are the extreme Far-Right and Rightist leaning right-wing politicians and political parties, in prominent European countries and in U.S.A, particularly after the Paris terror attacks and massacre in U.S. city of San Bernardino (both incident happen in 2015) the right-wing politicians determinedly in hyper active mood started delivering hard hitting spirited speeches. Political extremists takes opportunity to further polarize the political system and society, uses opportunity to divide people, now we all know the past history, what **Napoleon Bonaparte and Adolf Hitler** did, they were destructive elements and destroyed major part of Europe, so this are historic facts, ambitious and eager political extremist are hero's for small section of society whom a small but significantly strong section of society feels and believes he/she (political extremist or a rightist leaning politician) is a messiah and will save them from evil, but another large section of society considers political extremist as an opportunist politician and a monster.

France, Britain, Russia and U.S. are all heavily nuclear armed nations, **wrong person for a right job**, if in modern times, an extremist hothead person in any of these nuclear armed country succeeds in occupying highest political office, becomes President or Prime-minister of any one of these country or in more than one of these countries, with his or her fingers on nuclear button, such an irresponsible frivolous person could create a havoc, and potentially destroy humanity.

Therefore, Islam in itself is dangerous evil, but, Islamophobia is even bigger and more devastating evil. Distinct dislike for Islam and Islamic people by majority of non-Muslim population of our world, growing religious intolerance, frustration is an common emotional reaction, therefore in anger and disappointment in many countries systematically brainwashed people are recklessly helping evil of another type, and through electoral process in elections by voting for the so-called ultra nationalist political parties, people are conveniently handing political power to wrong person or persons.

I once overheard someone saying, "The entire human Civilization will collapse, if Oil Wells runs dry."

What is so significant about it? Why is petroleum crude oil & gas so important for us (humans)? Yes, indeed, it's very important, because your "Footwear, underwear and cookware" every wear and ware contains crude oil in it?

Whenever the topic for discussion is Crude oil & gas, one particular region of world and its people comes to everyone's mind, Yep, they are the Arabs, and the Persian Gulf and Arabian Peninsula region of the world.

Outside the Arab world most people have this popular misconception that because there is massive petroleum crude oil reserves in Middle-east Arabian countries, therefore by default every Arab citizen is Rich and wealthy, No that's not true, yes, there are many Arabs in the Mid-east Arabian countries who are exceptionally wealthy, but those folks who have wealth have got less to do with oil but more to do with their business acumen and skills, while many individual Arabs are rich because they are well connected with political hierarchy and have direct access to ruling political families, but significantly large percentage of population in countries like Iraq, Saudi Arabia, Yemen, Syria, Jordan and Egypt etc are economically backwards and considered poor, also historically the unemployment rate has stubbornly remain high in several Arabian countries, unemployment rate in many Arabian countries have for decades remain in higher Double-Digit."

One common question, which most people eagerly ask is, why do Western countries as well as Chinese and Japanese take keen interest in Persian Gulf and Arabian countries internal matters? Is it all because of Oil or are there some other interest and reasons attached? The answer is, not really Oil & Gas, its true in 1970s and 1990s the Western countries and Japanese were overwhelmingly dependent on supplies of Oil & gas from the Arab countries situated in the mid-east Asia, but equation changed because in the 21st century petroleum Oil & gas has been discovered in many other parts of the world, large reserves of oil and gas has been discovered and are being commercially exploited, between 2004 and 2013 many new petroleum oil and gas fields were discovered in many different parts of the world chiefly in countries in Central-Asia, Africa and South-America, but also the U.S.A the largest and biggest consumer of oil in the world has discovered huge quantity of oil and gas in its own backyard, new age modern technology called **"Fracking" to explore Shale Oil & Gas from deep under the surface by brutally cracking the Rocks** has helped U.S.A greatly in achieving energy self-sufficiency. Additional supplies of Crude Oil from many Non-Arab countries and also increase use of Biofuel and renewable energy in several countries, all combination of reasons have made U.S and European nations less concern and less dependent of Oil & gas supplies from Persian gulf countries.

In 1980s and 90s, the Arab countries use to have immense clout and use to often intimidate other alleged unfriendly non-abiding countries of dire consequences, and threaten to disrupt the supply of crude oil with an intention to sabotage their economy, the oil rich Arab countries no longer have leverage, and their influence has receded considerably, as there is enough oil & gas available from alternate sources.

This is very crucial because it provides us perspective of what **"Power of Money"** does and can do, how potent is power of money? Let us get understanding of it.

The U.S, West-European nations, Japanese and Chinese are not particularly interested in petroleum Oil from Arab countries, they take extreme and keen interest in Arab countries because it provides the western corporates large consumer market to sell their products and services, it is the money that many Arab countries earns from selling petroleum oil in international market is what matters most to the Americans, Europeans, Chinese and Japanese governments and their corporates, their businesses and companies sells everything to the Arab consumers, the Arabs buys Food items and Medicines, Automobiles and Aircrafts, Collection of Arts and Paintings, Fancy clothes and perfumes, arms and ammunition, fighter jets and ships.

For U.S and its allies (the west-Europeans and Japanese) on one side and the Chinese and Russians on the other side, what extravagantly matters most to both faction and sides is their business and commercial interest to gain enormous Business Profits, that's the absolute reason, why they take keen interest in the Persian and Arabian countries.

When a Person or a country have immense Power of Money, obviously they'll also have incredible Purchasing power to buy and to purchase many different items and products, so, when a Person or a country/countries or for that matter anyone and anybody who has/have solid Purchasing power, hence many people and business owners by choice or by compulsion will follow that particular Person/persons to sell them and to convince them to buy many different items and products. This is why "Power of Money" is the greatest Power a person or a country can have, and this is precisely the reason why so many people around the World so desperately needs money.

Money-money-money; money arguably is each humans top priority, few people in world have lots of money, but, lots of people in world have less money or no money.

The reasons why there's chaos and troubles in many Muslim ruled countries and in Muslim dominated countries, it is because of economic backwardness, with large Muslim population socially and economically backwards, in Muslim dominated countries like Afghanistan, Pakistan, Bangladesh, Tunisia, Egypt, Somalia and many more countries there is high level of unemployment and or underemployment, big majority of people find it difficult to find jobs, so people have less or no money in their pockets, but at the same time rising prices of essentials are increasing cost of living, day to day expenses are rising but earning opportunities are dwindling.

Religion holds back progress, who has failed whom? "Has their religion (Islam) failed Muslims or Muslim folks have failed their religion?" it is their religion (Islam) that has failed Muslims.

Backwardness no development, no new industrial projects, no plan of new business investments, all is not well in Muslim ruled countries, millions of Muslim families living and surviving in desperate poverty, can't simply blame terrorism and corruption for all the failures in many Muslim ruled countries.

Muslim folks loyalty is only with their religion and not with humanity, people live life to serve purpose of their religion and care less to serve purpose of humanity, callous and arrogant Muslim community but particularly the Sunni Muslim community without any remorse and regrets publically calls every Non- Sunni Muslim religious communities and people as Kafir (infidels) and considers infidels as evil, and Sunni Muslims are of the view that harming infidels in any which manner is their mandated holy duty, Sunnis endeavour is to have this world free of Kafirs (infidels) by any which means possible.

Secular peace loving and liberals considers jihadists elements as terrorists and monsters, but for the Sunni Muslim community those members of their community who joins jihadists group and becomes a jihadi, the Jihadists are considered sacred and for Sunnis whosoever is a jihadi is part of Islamic army and duty of Islamic army is to wipe out all those people and everything in world that is non-Islamic.

It is often debated and discussed at length in public places as well in media, that it is oil money that is funding and aiding Sunni jihadist forces, many political analysts blame and accuses the wealthy oil rich Sunni Arab countries like the Saudis, Qataris and Kuwaitis for funding and financing Sunni extremism and terrorism, it is alleged that most of the Islamic schools and institutions in many different countries are funded by wealthy oil rich Arab countries, and Islamic schools and institutions are perfect breeding ground for radicalization process, young boys and girls are brainwashed, are incited and encouraged to take up Guns and Explosive materials in their hands and do not show any remorse and not to hesitate one bit firing and blasting Non-Sunni Muslim people anywhere in the world so as to fulfil their beloved prophet dream and Islamic god "Allah's" order to establish complete Islamic rule all over the world.

Many medieval Muslim thinkers, overwhelmingly pursue strong Islamist agenda, in mostly Muslim dominated countries young Sunni Muslim boys and girls are prevented from pursuing modern era graduate studies and university studies, schools and institutions in few of the Islamic countries are often brutally attacked, schools and universities in Pakistani city of Peshawar often comes under attack, terrorists brutally killing teachers and students inside schools and universities classrooms.

Insular belief and mind-set as well as rigid attitude, large population not willing to change with times are some of the uncanny reasons for social and economic backwardness and also for political instability in many Muslim countries.

Massive fall in prices of petroleum oil and gas since the middle of year 2014, some political analysts thought and felt will help dent Islamic terrorism because the large oil and gas producing Sunni Arab countries will earn lot less money, crude oil prices falling from the high of $115 per barrel in first half of 2014 to as low as $28 per barrel in January-2016, but on the contrary the Sunni militants and terrorists attacks and activities further increased since 2014, Sunni terrorists vigorously have been targeting and attacking non-Sunni Muslim targets around the world.

Steepest fall in oil prices, oil and gas producing Arab nations are in quandary, because of escalating violence and civil wars in many Islamic countries also because of Islamic sectarian strife, it is difficult to ascertain the fact as in due to massive drop in oil prices if the once cash rich Arabs still have cash dollars in hands or not, whatsoever maybe the truth about Arab's finances, but one thing is evident that due to major disturbance and increased terrorism in Islamic world, the cash rich Arab countries like Saudi Arabia, Qatar and Kuwait are forced to increase their defence budget, squeeze on resources, the Sunni Arab countries but also Shia ruled Iraq have to spend more money buying arms and ammunitions, sharp increases in defence expenditure, all this means that Arabs are earning lot less money but have to spend lot more money on buying arms, food and medicines, plus at same time they also have to take care of their respective country's citizens social security and welfare.

Disastrous fall in prices of petroleum oil and gas has or will force countries like Iraq and Saudi Arabia to borrow more money from international financial markets to finance their increase expenditure, which will increase Arab countries sovereign debt and if oil prices sustains lower levels for longer period of time, in which case all Arab countries will have to drastically reduce subsidies and cut benefits that they've long been providing their citizens and will be compel to raise local taxes, this is fearful situation an imminent risk that increase in taxes on citizens and massive cut in subsidies will further jeopardize the Islamic world and cause more civilian unrest and create political instability. Also because in good times these wealthy Sunni Arab countries Saudi Arabia, Qatar, Kuwait provides large financial aid and grants and financial support to many impoverish Sunni Muslim dominated countries like Pakistan, Bangladesh and North-Sudan etc, if oil revenue falls and income declines in which case Arabs won't be in position to provide prodigious financial support to other chiefly Sunni Muslim countries and will be unable fund various social and religious Islamic institutions.

There are dual effects felt for everything that's substantive, the stronger you become the more vulnerable you are, when an individual person or be it a country, becomes rich and wealthy, the power of wealth makes a person or the country's ruling administration restless and insane, on the other side poverty as well makes person/persons or a country increasingly frustrated and feeble, so, being influential rich and wealthy, or, being poor and stricken, both types of situation are dangerous; This is what has happen or is happening with **Islam**, as, Islam the religion and the follower of Islam have for long been of delusional view that they are incredibly strong force and that they have sufficient muscle and money power to take over the whole world, by all means at their disposal. The real problem is which seemingly have created bigger problems for the world as well is that, Islam and its followers the Muslims have made tremendous fundamental mistake in overestimating their ability and capacity to destroy everything that is non-Islamic in this world, and even bigger blunder the Islamic folks have made is that they gravely underestimated the striking capacity and financial strength and power of non-Islamic communities,

The firm belief among Muslim is, if the entire Sunni Islam unites, then they can certainly achieve their objective of establishing Islamic caliphate all over the world and that no one can stop them from conquering the whole world. Precisely this is the reason that almost every-day you listen the Islamic clerics and jihadist terrorists threatening the world's non-Muslim population of dire consequences if any one dares to become obstacle.

The unfounded belief of Islamic folks, has made the entire Sunni-Muslim community arrogant and their overconfidence has made them more vulnerable, Muslim brothers and sisters are wasting huge financial resources and human lives.

Muslims have brazen double standards, while Sunni-Muslims mince no words, and without any regret and shame calls every non-Sunni Muslim communities and those people who do not believe in Islamist doctrine as **Kafir** (infidels), an according to Islamic doctrine Kafirs (infidels) are evil worshippers, and according to hardline Islamist belief harming and punishing or even going to an extent of killing the infidels is considered as holy duty of every practicing devout Muslim, Muslim clerics and priests on record preach and advices to followers of Islam that everything that is produced by non-Islamic communities or atheists (unbelievers) is Haraam (illegitimate), hence Muslims should restrain themselves from using and consuming foods items and many other consumer products and material that are produced by Pagan, Jewish and other non-believers of Islam.

You may listen such slogans in most of the Islamic countries as well in Muslim dominated countries and localities, Muslims shouting death to America, boycott Israel, Muslims are severely critical towards Jewish community, and also we hear from Muslims many other slogans condemning non-Muslims and idol worshippers, but, members of Muslim communities and followers of Islam when they are wounded and injured or suffering from illness to heal their wounds and to cure diseases they consume medicines which apparently are researched and developed by Jewish scientists, and manufactured in Jewish or Pagan (idol and nature worshipers) owned factories. Muslims makes extensive use of scientific technologies which again are researched, design and developed by Jewish or atheists and most likely manufactured in Jewish or Christian owned factories.

Similarly Islamic countries and Muslim institutions graciously accept economic and financial aid and help from non-Islamic countries governments (U.S.A., Japan and European governments provides Billions of Dollars in economic aid and other incentives to so many Islamic and Muslim dominated countries) and financial institutions, so accepting money and donations from financial institutions which are controlled by Jewish or atheists is OK for Muslim folks, seeking asylum and refuge in non-Islamic country is OK, but, yet Muslims are not ready to concede, they continue pouring stream of invective against non-Sunni Muslim communities, Muslims will take money, accept economic aid packages from non-Muslim governments and institutions and use their technology and consume medicines, yet Muslims brazenly calls non-Muslim communities "Kafir" (infidel) and vociferate for total destruction of unbelievers or to say they (Sunni-Muslims) vow to eliminate and destroy anyone and everything that is non-Islamic.

Extremely clever, cunning and crafty is how I would describe the Islamic jihadi army hierarchy or bosses whosoever these mysterious people are, the strategy of the Jihadis or to say Islamist army is to traumatize the world's non-Sunni Muslim population, instead of challenging rival enemies army in open battle field for full frontal confrontation and for decisive outcome, they've adopted more subtle combative strategy, efficiently fighting low key war, the Sunni jihadists and terrorist groups by frequently targeting and attacking non-Sunni Muslim population whenever and wherever in so many different parts of the world, it proves more cost effective and above all more damaging and harming. Sporadic terror attacks at strategic locations exerts tremendous psychological pressure on non-Muslim countries governments as well on common-people.

Islamic sectarian strife, wars in Islamic countries, poverty in Muslim dominated Asian and African countries, all these combination of reasons creates more humanitarian reason and excuse for Muslims to migrate and populate European and American countries. Here is another perspective, the Islamic jihadi forces and terrorists in 18th, 19th and 20th century have firmly consolidated its position and have strengthen its bases in much of Asian and African continents, it seems obvious in 21st century Islamist Jihadists are prying to takeover European continent, the allege strategy of Islamic jihadists commanders would be to terrorize the mainstream European society, sporadic deadly terror attacks hitting prominent European towns and cities, would potentially severely hurt Europe's economy, create fear in minds of Europeans and cause sense of insecurity. Europeans seeing rise in Islamic numbers and increase in Muslim population inside Europe, feeling enormous pressure at least some of the frustrated Europeans will be *compel to leave Europe for good* and move to other safer destination outside European continent for safe and secured life, this is precisely what the Islamic Jihadi army commanders would like the most because that's exactly what they would want to happen, as it will increase Muslim population and decrease European population, after all politics is all about numbers, with rise in Muslim population it will make Sunni-Muslims task easier to gain total and comprehensive control of Europe.

Something similar happened in Africa, when Muslims were systematically gaining control of many African countries, the non-Muslim Black people under duress and frustration moved out of Africa and migrated to countries in Europe or America.

Again the same question arises; Does "Petro-dollars" funds Islamic terrorism and extremism? Western media and politicians for decades have been complaining that the wealthy oil rich Sunni Arab countries such as Saudi Arabia, Qatar and Kuwait have been promoting and generously funding Islamic extremism and terrorism, so it is alleged that several prominent Muslim countries governments have been helping and promoting jihadist (Islamic holy-warriors) groups. It maybe be perception of many but perhaps not a reality. Perhaps, I would say its partially true that couple of Sunni Arab countries earning large amount of money selling petroleum oil & gas uses some amount of the oil income to fund Islamic extremism and terrorism, but as it is that no criminal gang or terrorist group can possibly sustain itself unless they've political patronage and until such time that they enjoy support of particular dominant ethnic or religious community. Therefore Sunni jihadist terrorism can't survive for a moment more unless they are backed and aided by their community members, clerics and political leaders.

There is a perception, and also true, can't deny the fact that there is **State sponsor terrorism**, wherein government of particular country for strategic reasons and for larger interest and benefit of their country they do finance extremist and terrorist groups, but it is equally true the other way around as well, which is that many criminal gangs and terrorist groups as well supports States by providing financial and other material help to governments and contributes significant amount of money for the welfare of people belonging to their own religious community.

Terrorism have been institutionalized, criminal syndicates and cartels as well as terrorist groups mobilize resources and finances from many different ways and means, Crime and Corruption have unofficially gained Industry Status. So talking about Islamic extremism and terrorism, Islamic terror and criminal enterprises, gangs and syndicates earns money and generates cash from many different means and are in position to fund governments and give big political donations to influential political leaders and political parties.

Sunni jihadist groups like "ISIS, Al Qaeda, Al Shabaab, Boko Haram," and many more fringe terror groups are allegedly involved in many illicit business and trade, while Africa based terror groups like Al Shabaab and Boko Haram, earns big amount of money to fund their jihadist project mainly through Poaching and killing wildlife in African forest and jungles and trade in endanger animals skins, bones and ivory, also earns money from illegal mining of minerals and extortion, seeking donations forcing people to donate money for Islamic causes which obviously is for jihad (Islam holy-war).

Similarly other terrorist groups like ISIS, Al Qaeda and Taliban and other criminal gangs mostly operating in west-Asia's Arabian countries, Afghanistan and Pakistan are allegedly involve in many unlawful and illegal business and trade such as "human trafficking, drug trafficking, trafficking in human organs, fake currency, counterfeit medicines, cybercrime, gambling and illegal betting and match fixing." So reverse is true as well with hundreds of billions of dollars they earn from all kinds of illicit and illegal business and trade, many of the criminal gangs and terrorist groups finance and funds also bribes the governments and government officials of many countries.

When topic of discussion is Islamic terrorism, one name that comes in minds of many of us and that name is **Osama Bin Laden**, Laden the allege founder of terror group Al Qaeda who became symbol of Sunni Islam jihad. Decades after the collapse of great **Ottoman Empire** in 1918/19 after the end of WWI, apparently it was Osama Laden who in 21st century revived struggle for establishing **Sunni Islam Caliphate** which means Sunni-Islam rule the world over. Especially in western world in Europe and America people know Osama bin laden as dreaded jihadist or terrorist, but wait a moment there is another man seriously associated with global Islamic jihad and he is a phenomenon in crime world and his name is **Dawood Ibrahim** who perhaps is more rich and resourceful than Osama bin laden was, Dawood Ibrahim an Indian born most prolific and high-profile international criminal, Dawood fled India in mid-1980s because for the brutal crimes he had committed hence he was wanted in many criminal cases, so as to avoid his arrest and he also feared of him being killed by rival criminal gangs so he left India and since than established his base in Dubai and Pakistani port city of Karachi.

Dawood Ibrahim arguably the most successful and influential gangster extremely wealthy and powerful who is supposedly worth billions of dollars, a very popular person enjoys celebrity status in south and west-Asia, **The Don** or **Bhai** (Brother) as he is popularly called and his criminal gang known as **D-Company**, Dawood Ibrahim's allege illegal business interest are "Contract killings, illegal betting and match fixing, drug trafficking, fake currency and financing Bollywood (Hindi films) movies and distribution," and many more illicit businesses and criminal activities deeply rooted throughout the world. Money earned by Dawood Ibrahim through criminal activities are then through frontend companies invested in many other mainstream businesses like Hotels, airlines, properties and stock-markets. It is alleged that Dawood is a principle financer of various Islamic terrorist groups largely operating in Pakistan and Afghanistan and when in need many Muslim nation governments in south-Asia and west-Asia seeks financial help from Dawood.

Dawood Ibrahim may have fled India to never possibly return back, but his heart remains in country of his birth, majority population in Indian sub-continent countries and in west-Asia passionately love watching Bollywood films (Hindi movies) and take keen interest in playing and watching their favourite sport **Cricket**, so does Dawood Ibrahim as well have great love and passion for Cricket and it is primarily through Cricket and Bollywood film industry Dawood has maintain close link with India and his compatriots, Dawood also have serious business interest in India as well because many of his close friends and business associates as well his siblings and relatives are living in India, Dawood Ibrahim allegedly pays generous amount of money to Indian politicians and bureaucrats and he finances election campaigns of many prominent Indian political parties. So in all not only Osama bin laden, but Dawood Ibrahim as well is a master strategist, clever and shrewd good at manoeuvring business deals, he's a prominent personality working and helping insensitive cause of his religion Sunni-Islam,

Many source of funding available for "**Islamic Jihadi Project**," to spread Islam and to destroy western and eastern Pagan culture and civilization, apart from earning money from ivory trade, drugs and people trafficking and all other sort of criminal activities and illegal trade that generates revenue for Islam's narcissistic plan of establishing Islamic rule all over the world, "**Vicious snake**" as some say the economically and socially progressive western countries are feeding snake which is ultimately going to venomously bite and diminish them, here I am referring to Europeans and Americans, several prominent Sunni-Muslim countries such as "Egypt, Afghanistan, Turkey, Pakistan, Jordan, Bangladesh" are major recipient of massive economic and humanitarian aid principally from non-Islamic western countries such as U.S.A., Britain and European Union, Tens of billions of dollar worth of financial package and soft loans are given to these Islamic countries, the frequent economic and humanitarian help is provided for the purpose to create public infrastructure, for healthcare and women empowerment, the economic help is for the **human-development** and to boost industrial activity so as to create jobs and business opportunities which would help to alleviate poverty.

Besides economic aid, U.S.A. Britain and France also have defence pact signed with many Islamic countries especially with Sunni majority Islamic countries, high-level of corruption in almost every country that receives massive financial aid, maximum amount of money allegedly is siphoned and gets transferred in personal bank accounts of corrupt politicians and bureaucrats, only a fraction of amount is spend for real purpose that is for the welfare and benefit of local citizens and also significantly large amount of money is allegedly diverted for Islamic causes meaning funds are transferred to the Jihadi accounts for them to use money for day-to-day expenses and for paying salaries to the Jihadis and to launch terror attacks on non-Muslims. As part of defence deal and defence pact the advance combative training that western military experts provides to the mainstream army personnel and soldiers, later on most of the weapons are than allegedly handed over to the Muslim Brotherhood backed Jihadists who use arms and military expertise to fight Jihad and religious wars against the non-Sunni Muslim communities.

So as it is that vicious Islamists are using significant amount of resources "cash-money, weapons and military training," that they acquire from the powerful western countries such as America, Britain and France and also some amount of monetary help and weapons from Russia, is used extensively by the Islamists to fight protracted religious wars and to strengthen their religion Sunni Islam.

Hundreds of thousands of people from Islamic countries migrating or are forced to migrate to western countries, escalating tension and unending sectarian conflicts, people smugglings and human trafficking became thriving business, but, where do these people get money to reach the shores of Europe? People are so desperately poor in Muslim countries they are literally starving therefore it is impossible for us to believe that these folks would have thousands of dollars in their pocket to pay the people smugglers, so, who is funding these desperately poor people to migrate to Europe? Obviously *"there is more to it than meets the eye,"* one theory is that the wealthy oil rich Sunni nations are financing the project **"Mass Muslim Migration"** to Europe obviously to heavily populate Europe and later America with Sunni Islamist folks so that later on it will become easy for them to establish Sunni Islam rule in these western countries without much bloodbath, other bigger perspective is and there is widespread outrageous speculation in social media that it is a prominent Jewish investment banker and few of his rich and influential friends are funding the Mass migration of Sunni Muslims to Europe and north-America for selfish long term Jewish interest and commercial interest, businesses are making oodles of money, stock-markets around the world between 2013 and 2016 are booming trading at historic high levels mainly because of unrelenting protracted war on terror and sectarian conflicts in Islamic world which is/has created demand for many products primarily defence equipment and military hardware and also unprecedented demand for food and medicines and advance communication devices. Terrorists are killing poor people on the streets and few thousand rich or to say super rich individuals with their family are enjoying life in their staggeringly beautiful homes enjoys sumptuous vacations at exotic locales.

Much like the same as it was widely reported in section of media that it were influential rich businessmen and rich Jewish bankers who all had orchestrated **World War 2** for a purpose. **Adolf Hitler** was just a mere puppet he was simply doing what few influential people subtly were dictating him to do, so, it is alleged, that, "Hitler" was merely following the order of his masters, real power was in someone else's hand. For selfish commercial interest and to obtain superlative political and economic power to rule the world, handful of them just few people who all wants to dominate the entire world's population, such crafty individual people manipulates and rig the system to their advantage.

There are allegations and charges that most of the European and American corporates and rich individuals pay lot less tax on their annual income.

Large MNC (multinational corporations) have always been accused of paying to little Tax in the country where they do business or have their company's head-quarter based, well, these large MNC are per se doing no wrong, it is just that they are taking advantage of favourable economic policy, if a particular country's tax laws are lenient and rules flexible, they opt to set up their company's head-quarter or subsidiary in that country, it is the government of any particular country is to be blamed if at all, because the government and politicians to compete with other peer nations and to boost profile of their country drafts incredibly favourable tax policy and provides other incentives to attract investments in their country, in interest of people of their country for creating jobs and business opportunities they levy lower tax or there also are countries which are absolute tax free so that more MNC and other small businesses can operate their business activity from their country.

Apart from terrorism and extremism another bigger problem and unprecedented challenge before Europeans and Americans is increase unemployment and underemployment, degree holder youngsters have no other choice but to accept low-skill low paying job or any kind of temporary work, manufacturing sector is down and out, maximum manufacturing have moved to other low-cost densely populated countries such as Pakistan, Bangladesh, Philippines, Vietnam and of course China, but manufacturing is gradually moving out of China as well to other low-cost producing nations, causing more pain to the Chinese, manufacturing industries have all but disappeared from Europe and America, and those industrial manufacturing units that still exist are **state-of-art-technology** fully automated therefore no new job opportunities are available, between 1985 till 2010 service sector and healthcare sector were thriving in Europe and America and had created millions of high paying jobs, but service and healthcare sector as well showing signs of fatigue, and experiencing remarkable slowdown, with advent of new age technology, and much needed **Internet revolution**, have changed things dramatically, service and healthcare sectors aren't creating more jobs instead hundreds of thousands of job losses are reported, most of the work is done or happens automatically, "Cloud computing technology, artificial intelligence, robotic technology, smart software," all such new age technologies enables companies to hire less staff, because they need less people to do work. Online payments, online trading in stocks and commodities, online ticket booking for railways and airplane, what more? Even the ever so reliable **retail sector** is as well losing steam, e-retailers providing option of online shopping sells products of daily consumption at lot more affordable rates, therefore many brick and mortar retailers on high-streets in Russia, Britain, U.S.A and many other European countries are compel to close their shops and stores, so in modern times most of the work happens online all kinds of information can be access and data transfer online, therefore no new jobs created instead people who have job are no longer secured and risk losing their job any moment, such high is risk uncertain situation is or has become more uncertain.

Substantial increase in crime rates besides racial and religious tension in Europe and America, increase risk of terrorism and extremism, petty crimes like pickpocketing and shoplifting to more organized crimes such as Bank robbery and looting is rampant, incidents of sexual violence, it is alleged and has been reported daring uncultured migrants from Islamic countries do not spare young children --- girls age 5 and 8 years are also targeted and molested in full public view, all such unsavoury news discourages many in Asia and people from other parts of the world to avoid travelling to Europe to spend their holidays instead explore other options and plan trip to new places which are more safe and secured and artistic as well affordable, so in Europe all sectors be it service sector, retail sector or tourism industry all are brutally affected and becomes another reason for increase in crime rates if people have nothing better or constructive things to do in life they enter perilous crime world.

Extraordinary economic slowdown and social problems in Europe and to some extent in America and also other countries like Egypt and Turkey, will help west-African nations, countries like "Namibia, Angola, Ghana, Botswana" can take advantage of deteriorating social and economic situation in Europe and Islamic countries to promote their respective country as new tourist destination and also provide other investment opportunities in mining and manufacturing, another country Argentina is beautiful country hence needs to take advantage to promote its tourism sector, and another country with lot of potential is **Iran,** Persians offer many new opportunities, Persia yet unexplored, lot of potential for cultural tourism, excellent food and hospitable environment, friendly people, so, there are lot of other countries which needs to be taken seriously, there is lot of untapped pool of potential tech-talent, for 3 decades (between 1980s until 2015) the Europeans and Americans have spent or rather wasted lot of time and money in India and China, most of the investments in these two countries are unyielding and less productive, Europeans and American businesses reckless investments in India have only destroyed wealth of Europeans, many in Europe and U.S. are deprived of cash money and have helped millions of Indians obtain unprecedented wealth, while many citizens of rich industrialized Europe and America or for that matter even in Arab countries became poor and are experiencing decline in living standards, many people and families in India became rich obtained massive wealth.

Islamic problems creates many more problems for others, Islamic sectarian and religious wars whether or not they're genuine or sham, has/have destabilize entire world and created social and economic problems.

To define Islam and its followers the Muslims, the critics and opponents of Islam describe "Islam is brutal religion and thoroughly chaotic," the sympathizers and supporters of Islam says "Islam is humble and peaceful religion," people are free to say and speak "what they feel and like."

But as we unbiasedly assess Islam, it is so that, "Muslims ruthlessly harm others and creates problems for others (non-Muslims)," also true is "Muslims harms fellow Muslims and creates more problems for themselves and for their communities," talking about growing violence world over, Islamist terrorists killing innocent people, true as it is evident, but there's another bigger perspective, just think again, Islamic extremists and terrorists kills and harm more Muslims than anyone else, yes maximum victims of brutal Islamic terrorism are their own "Muslims," Sunni jihadists and also Islamic countries official army and security forces not only kills more Muslims but they also destroy livelihood of Millions of Muslims.

Islam is religion brutally divided into two faction "**Shia** and **Sunni**," and it will be worth noting that all terribly inhuman and devastatingly dangerous terrorist groups such as "ISIS, Al Qaeda, Boko Haram, Taliban, Al Shabaab" and so many more such jihadi groups owe their allegiance to <u>Sunni Islam</u>, Islamic terrorism is culture of Sunni Islam.

There are many perspective but bigger perspective is religion, there is too much confusion in minds of many as to <u>whether or not</u> all three supposedly Abrahamic religions <u>Judaism, Christianity and Islam</u> follows the same god, a very crucial but always a controversial topic to debate, devout followers of Islam's unfounded beliefs, stubborn as they (Muslims) are not establishing the truth of their religion.

Muslim people are thoroughly misinformed and seriously misguided by astute Muslim clerics and priests, using unprecedented tactics to systematically brainwash the Muslim population and to entice and encourage the gullible non-Muslims to embrace Islam and force them to pledge allegiance to their beloved Prophet Muhammad, the Muslim clerics and priests preaches the alleged message of their prophet to the followers of Islam, they in their discourse and sermons says, **"There is only one God and that god is Allah, you (Muslims) who follow Islam are the best creatures of Allah (Islamic God), and Allah loves you all and the remaining non-believers are Kafir (Infidels), and with regards to Infidels -- Muslims are thought to believe that God made serious mistake in creating non-Islamic religious communities therefore they (people who do not follow Sunni-Islam) are flawed and worse creatures hence they will burn in fire of Hell, so they (Islamic clerics) preach and assures Muslims that "<u>Paradise for Sunni-Muslims and fire of hell for non-Muslims</u>."**

There is it seems a deliberate attempt to polarize global civil society and to divide world's population on religious and cultural lines, the Sunni-Muslim population world over as of 2016 is approximately 1.2 Billion, with Sunni Islam on one side of the divide and the rest on the other side and leave nothing in between, so, this is why I say "**Islam versus the rest.**" Islam have nothing much to lose so they are not losing much, by creating nightmarish and chaotic situation for non-Sunni Muslim population all over the world, Islam only have something to gain so they are gaining a lot (economic and political power).

With major parts and large territories in Asia and Africa already under Islamic control, all eyes are on what will be the next move of the Islamists in Europe! Will Islam succeed in conquering Europe? And if Islam by any chance does succeed in its plan of capturing political power in Europe than sky will be the limit, Islam will then rule the world. Or, will **Islam implode**? What if the Islamic people themselves destroy Islam?

The Muslim institutions and religious council hierarchy, clerics and politicians for generations have successfully indoctrinated minds of naïve and gullible individuals; here in an interesting article to have better and scientific perspective of who Allah (the Muslim God) actually is and what is its significance Article title **"Allah – The Moon God" The Archeology of the Middle East**"- "The religion of Islam has as its focus of worship a deity by the name of *"Allah."* The Muslims claim that Allah in pre-Islamic times was the biblical God of the Patriarchs, prophets, and apostles. The issue is thus one of continuity. Was *"Allah"* the biblical God or a pagan god in Arabia during pre-Islamic times? The Muslim's claim of continuity is essential to their attempt to convert Jews and Christians for if *"Allah"* is part of the flow of divine revelation in Scripture, then it is the next step in biblical religion. Thus we should all become Muslims. But, on the other hand, if Allah was a pre-Islamic pagan deity, then its core claim is refuted. Religious claims often fall before the results of hard sciences such as archeology. We can endlessly speculate about the past or go and dig it up and see what the evidence reveals. This is the only way to find out the truth concerning the origins of Allah. As we shall see, the hard evidence demonstrates that the god Allah was a pagan deity. In fact, he was the Moon-god who was married to the sun goddess and the stars were his daughters.

Archaeologists have uncovered temples to the Moon-god throughout the Middle East. From the mountains of Turkey to the banks of the Nile, the most wide-spread religion of the ancient world was the worship of the Moon-god. In the first literate civilization, the Sumerians have left us thousands of clay tablets in which they described their religious beliefs. As demonstrated by Sjoberg and Hall, the ancient Sumerians worshipped a Moon-god who was called many different names. The most popular names were Nanna, Suen and Asimbabbar. His symbol was the crescent moon. Given the amount of artifacts concerning the worship of this Moon-god, it is clear that this was the dominant religion in Sumeria. The cult of the Moon-god was the most popular religion throughout ancient Mesopotamia. The

Assyrians, Babylonians, and the Akkadians took the word Suen and transformed it into the word Sin as their favorite name for the Moon-God. As Prof. Potts pointed out, *"Sin is a name essentially Sumerian in origin which had been borrowed by the Semites."*

In ancient Syria and Canna, the Moon-god Sin was usually represented by the moon in its crescent phase. At times the full moon was placed inside the crescent moon to emphasize all the phases of the moon. The sun-goddess was the wife of Sin and the stars were their daughters. For example, Istar was a daughter of Sin. Sacrifices to the Moon-god are described in the Pas Shamra texts. In the Ugaritic texts, the Moon-god was sometimes called Kusuh. In Persia, as well as in Egypt, the Moon-god is depicted on wall murals and on the heads of statues. He was the Judge of men and gods. The Old Testament constantly rebuked the worship of the Moon-god (Deuteronomy 4:19; 17:3; II Kings 21:3, 5; 23:5; Jeremiah 8:2; 19:13; Zephaniah 1:5, etc.) When Israel fell into idolatry, it was usually the cult of the Moon-god. As a matter of fact, everywhere in the ancient world, the symbol of the crescent moon can be found on seal impressions, steles, pottery, amulets, clay tablets, cylinders, weights, earrings, necklaces, wall murals, etc. In Tell-el-Obeid, a copper calf was found with a crescent moon on its forehead. An idol with the body of a bull and the head of man has a crescent moon inlaid on its forehead with shells. In Ur, the Stele of Ur-Nammu has the crescent symbol placed at the top of the register of gods because the Moon-god was the head of the gods. Even bread was baked in the form of a crescent as an act of devotion to the Moon-god. The Ur of the Chaldees was so devoted to the Moon-god that it was sometimes called Nannar in tablets from that time period.

A temple of the Moon-god has been excavated in Ur by Sir Leonard Woolley. He dug up many examples of moon worship in Ur and these are displayed in the British Museum to this day. Harran was likewise noted for its devotion to the Moon-god. In the 1950's a major temple to the Moon-god was excavated at Hazer in Palestine. Two idols of the Moon god were found. Each was a stature of a man sitting upon a throne with a crescent moon carved on his chest. The accompanying inscriptions make it clear that these were idols of the Moon-god. Several smaller statues were also found which were identified by their inscriptions as the "daughters" of the Moon-god. What about Arabia? As pointed out by Prof. Coon, *"Muslims are notoriously loath to preserve traditions of earlier paganism and like to garble what pre-Islamic history they permit to survive in anachronistic terms."...........*

The followers of Islam should stop blaming others for their misery, the truth is that Islamic folks are inspired by all the wrong things in life, the Islamic doctrine and theology is failing the Muslims.

Be good to others, expect others to be good to you.

Touching base with extreme realities of the so-called Abrahamic religions, when we talk of Islam, we always talk of its founder Muhammad, the so-called alleged last prophet of God "Muhammad" is discussed extensively, but, no one really discusses, as in, how Islam was formed? What made Muhammad so great and achieve unprecedented success? All talks of god sending his angel "**Gabriel**" down on earth to communique his message to Muhammad, and so many such imaginative and false stories, unscientific explanation and narratives that we listen and read, but these are all wild imagination and rubbish talks, no secular scholars and intellectuals will ever believe such nonsense theories and stories.

Here is a real true perspective in brief to understand *"how Islam came into being, and, what and who made Muhammad so popular and powerful person ever born on this planet,"* > Muhammad was born into low-income family in either Mecca or Medina modern day part of Saudi Arabia, he belonged to Banu Hashim clan which was part of Quraysh tribe a very powerful tribe in Medina, Muhammad remained unmarried single till he was 25years of age, he use to survive well doing odd job and business deals, even though Muhammad was an absolute illiterate, but it has been written about him that he had excellent oratory and negotiating skills, as it is said that "behind every successful man there is a woman," according to historians have recorded that in 595CE, he married Khadīja bint Khuwaylid and she apparently was 15 years older in age than him.

Khadija was also from same Quraysh tribe and was a successful businesswoman, she was a merchant and use to trade large consignment of goods and products, because of her business success she was very influential and respected throughout Arabian region, Khadija was rich, she had staggering personality was shrewd, intelligent, smart, compassionate, use to help and support many people, she was kind and generous woman, but, she did not believe and did not like worshipping idols, but she in her house use to have idol of **Al-Uzza**, "(**Al-'Uzzá** was one of the three chief goddesses of Arabian religion in pre-Islamic times and was worshiped by the pre-Islamic Arabs along with **Allāt** and **Manāt**)," so it was Muhammad's first wife Khadija significantly guided and helped Muhammad gain success, Islam is basically brainchild NOT OF Muhammad's but his first wife Khadija, Khadija was the first person to embrace Islam and she is the one who promoted him as prophet of the believers.

It so happened that during 6th and 7th century people of Arabia and Mesopotamia were fed-up of frequent wars and violence between various kingdoms and warlords, chaotic situation in the Arabian region, "poverty, persecution, high inflation and unemployment," had made people in the region restless as they were feeling insecure, the people wanted peace and a leader to lead them, and Muhammad's first wife being a successful businesswoman having trading business spread across Arabian and Mesopotamia region, hence she was well connected had good contacts in the region, her sources use to constantly update her with information regarding economic and political situation, she was widely travelled and intelligent woman, knew all about peoples aspiration and what is the mood of the people in Arabia and Mesopotamia region, when Khadija realized that people are disenchanted with the political leaders and kings who rule them, she seized an opportunity to exploit the than existing ground situation, and the generous woman that she (Khadija) was, instead of promoting herself and becoming leader and chieftain herself, she used all her resources and the goodwill she had among large majority of people for all her philanthropic work and help she had rendered to so many people, she used it all to her advantage and promoted her husband, she promoted Muhammad as prophet of the believers, and sometime in 610CE launched a peoples movement and named it **Islam** headed by her doting husband Muhammad, Islam was initially a peaceful movement project, majority of people of Hejaz (present day -- Saudi Arabia) liked new peace initiative and gracefully accepted Muhammad as their new leader, many unconditionally pledged allegiance to Muhammad, so Islam was initially started as peaceful movement and had given people a new hope. Muhammad till the time his first wife Khadīja bint Khuwaylid was alive remained loyal to her and did not had any other wife/wives or any extramarital affairs.

"(It is not clear, as to, how many biological children Muhammad had of his own? But, Muhammad for sure had one child from his first wife Khadija bint Khuwaylid had a beautiful daughter her name '**Fatima-Zahra**,' like mother like daughter, Fatima was beautiful, kind-hearted, brave and courageous woman, she married Muhammad's cousin **Ali ibn Abi Talib**, when after death of Muhammad there was rebellion in Islam over his succession and leadership issue, Fatima along with her husband Imam Ali founded **Shiite Islam**, yes, Fatima is founder of Shia Islam, she is mother of the followers of Shia Islam, she had two sons **Imam Hassan** and **Imam Hussein**; Fatima resolutely and vehemently opposed the Sunni caliph and Sunni-Islam terrorism)."

But sadly in 620CE Muhammad's first wife Khadija died, and after death of his first wife things dramatically began to change in Islam and unfortunately changed for the worse, till his first wife Khadija was alive Muhammad was disciplined and civilized person, was a very humble man, but soon after death of his first wife, Muhammad was corrupted, Muhammad started receiving advises from all the wrong people, Muhammad broke all his earlier promises and commitments he had made to people of Medina and Hejaz. Islam from peaceful movement became violent and corrupt, Islam became political movement and started attacking and looting villages and resorted to forceful conversions, in wars Islamic army started looting wealth and raping young women and girls, Muhammad himself became self-spoiled he started marrying one woman after another, some record suggest after death of his first wife Khadija, Muhammad married as many as 8 more women, most notable was his marriage to 6 year old kid the voracious **Aisha**, it has been said that he married Aisha when her age was 6 and consummated her when she was just 9 years old, apart from many wives Muhammad also had many concubines, Muhammad voraciously indulged in sex with many women, so initially as it was that Islam was a peaceful religion and its founder Muhammad was a humble man, but after the death of Muhammad's first wife Khadija neither Islam remained peaceful nor did Muhammad remained humble, it will be safe for us to assume "evil took control of both Islam and its founder **Muhammad**."

Man has/have created Religion and Religion has not created man. Religion is a man-made device designed to focus people's attention and energy on a single unchanging and uncompromising supreme being.

Religion/religions needs people for their survival, religions survive because of we people, and people per se do not need religion for their survival, we people can survive and be more happy and united without religions.

The power to manipulate beliefs is all that matters most, because we humans live with beliefs and it is always easy to manipulate beliefs.

In Germany Bavaria's finance minister, Markus Söder, said the German people "do not want a multicultural society" and recommended they should be sent back over the next three years. More than one million refugees have arrived in Germany over the past year, sparking backlash among critics of Chancellor Angela Merkel's open-door policy. Mr Söder said integration of those from different cultural backgrounds was "bound to fail." We know from history that the political right wing first emerged during the French Revolution. In 1789, at the États Généraux (legislative assembly of the different classes of French society), the pro-royalty group sat on the right of the president and the pro-labourer group sat on the left. what is generally called right wing or far right - often as a pejorative and not merely an identifier - is the tendency to strongly favour nationalism, be xenophobic, and draw from Christian religious values (sometimes resulting in anti-Semitism or Islamophobia). The right wing rhetoric claims that the economy of the country, the cultural values of the society, and social security benefits for natives are all under threat. Some of those on the right wing in Europe even feel that if they detach themselves from the European Union (EU), their problems would be solved. In the Netherlands, Geert Wilders, the founder and leader of the **Partij voor de Vrijheid** has been vocal against Islam for quite a number of years (for instance, he went as far as calling the Quran a fascist book, comparing it with Hitler's Mein Kampf). With the mounting refugee crisis, he is opposed to accepting any immigrants from the Islamic world. "Islam is a totalitarian ideology. Muslims are its victims. Just imagine you're a gay person in a Muslim family," Rightist Dutch politician **Geert Wilders wrote in his op-ed**. "the more Islamic apostates there are, the less misogyny, the less hatred of gays, the less anti-Semitism, the less oppression, the less terror and violence, and the more freedom there will be." And so it is in many European countries. **Alternative for Germany** (AfD), the German anti-Muslim party, is led by politicians with a strong social conservative background but has **moved left on gay rights** in recent years. Swedish far-rightists organized a **pride parade** going through Muslim neighborhoods, intending to highlight anti-gay attitudes in the Muslim community.

Pamela Geller, one of the most vociferous and vocal anti-Muslim writers in the US, **took out ads on San Francisco buses quoting anti-gay statements** by figures like Osama bin Laden and the Muslim Brotherhood's Yusuf al-Qaradawi, saying, "The ads will increase awareness about the subjugation and oppression of gays under Shariah law. The gay community should be standing with me, not against me."

With regards to gays and homosexuals, it is not just as if Islam have problems, but other religions as well have problems and disagree with same sex relationship and considers it as a **taboo** and a major problem to humanity, Judaism, Christianity and more conservative Pagan religions all have problems with gays and homosexuals.

Lobby culture has deep roots in American politics, **lobbyist**s lobby for their patron in corridors of power to seek political favours for their businesses or for their religion, it is alleged that American lawmakers are more loyal to the lobbyists than to their public. There exist the "Jewish Israeli & American lobby, wall-street lobby, arms manufacturers lobby but more prominent is **Sunni Arab lobby**," rich and wealthy powerful groups significantly influence government's decision making process, it has been reported that Saudi Arabia and Qataris major force behind Sunni Arab lobby in U.S.A., gives away massive political donations, presidential election campaigns are funded by rich business houses and dictatorial governments, in return for business and political favours, many lawmakers are privately funded or systematically bribed so to say. Something similar in European politics as well "Organized criminal gangs and mafias" allegedly funds many politicians and political parties, also religious communities such as Sunni Arabs it is alleged privately finance and donates significantly large amount of money to political parties, in return these corrupt politicians and government officials helps Islamic causes.

Far right rightists politicians as well as the leftists and socialists political parties simply exploits prevailing islamophobia and anti-Islam sentiments for their own personal ascendancy, highly provocative and spirited speeches at political events simply to gain power and rule the country, it actually helps Islamic causes massively when there is political turmoil and civilian unrest in any non-Muslim nation, the bitter tiff between socialists and far right political parties creates atmosphere of economic and political uncertainty which apparently weakens the country and divides the mainstream population, therefore be it in India, America or in Europe it has been observed that islamophobia and hate crimes against Muslims in real sense only further strengthens Islam, it unites the Sunni Muslims and divides the non-Muslims. Sharp divisions and polarization in society on cultural and religious lines is what the Muslim-brotherhood strategists wants, it will help Islam conquer the world.

Islamists are trying hard and have majorly succeeded in strengthening their bases inside Europe and America (both in' U.S., and Canada), growth of Islam and fearing threat to their civilization, **nationalists movement** is gaining momentum in Europe and America, corrupt liberal and secular governments are weakening and falling, *ultranationalists rightists politicians and political parties are or have seized an opportunity for themselves and are systematically instilling fear of Islam in minds of mainstream European population to gain politically and to capture political power*, be it in "Netherlands, Germany, France or Italy" between 2014 and 2016 there is spectacular rise in jingoism, crowd cheers politicians who speaks fearlessly against Islam and who detest Muslims, but will these rightists political extremists save the Europeans from brutal bloodthirsty Islamic forces who've entered Europe with simple goal and clear objective which is to conquer Europe and to establish Islamic sharia law in Europe and later in America. Or will these aggressive rightists political extremists further exacerbate the situation, pass legislations imposing stricter rules to govern and to discipline the Islamists, which would provoke the Islamists hence lead to more bloodbath on the streets of Europe and America and cause ultimate disintegration of Europe much to the liking of Islamic jihadi forces, that is what Muslim brotherhood game plan is to sabotage from within and total destruction of Europe and America and finally clear path for hoisting Islamic flag in Rome and in Washington.

Rightists leaning European population wants nothing less than complete ban on Islam, right-wing and Neo-Nazi wants Islamic mosques and Koranic studies be abandoned in Europe, and all Muslim immigrants be sent back to their respective Islamic countries, and same is the demand in U.S.A., and Canada as well, no special and preferential treatments to Muslims strict no to Halal food and Muslim women wear European style clothes.

Many Europeans are furious when they see increase number of African and Arab Muslims wandering around on the streets of European cities at public places in Parks or beaches and in restaurants, wherever you go in Europe thousands of African and Arab Muslims are present in large number, which makes the non-Muslim population feel jittery and especially scares young women and girls. Compelling many hot-head Europeans to react, rise in islamophobia, hate crimes against Islamists have increase, Muslims suffers extreme embarrassment and distress at times when they are mocked and abused, Muslims are looked upon as "**ancient aliens**," Islamists are branded as terrorists, "all you 'Muslims' are the same all you Muslims are terrorists," is what you might hear some impatient Europeans shouting at Muslims, starring at Muslim women who are donning Abaya, Burqa or Hijab, some news reports allegedly suggest Muslims are denied accommodation in hotels and some restaurant owners refuses to serve food to Muslims, at times Muslims are also abruptly asked to de-board from airplane and train fearing they are terrorists, well, I would say all this humiliation because since 622 AD Islamic folks have behaved and treated non-Muslims indifferently and humiliated them, Islamists are paying price for their own misdeed Muslims are thought from childhood not to respect non-Muslims because Islamic theology and doctrine teaches that non-Muslims are bad creation of god and are infidels hence are inferior and are as good as "**evil**," but no matter be it you are a Muslim or non-Muslim, after all we are all humans, Islamists are arrogant and misinformed have no comprehensive understanding of science and knows nothing about humanity and human evolution and even if they know it they ignore modern scientific teachings, so, if there is fundamental fault in Muslims, but, are others meaning non-Muslims any better? Is it the non-Muslim population of world is intelligent? No ---- not at all.

Excerpts from article **"Islamophobia fueled by right-wing politics and propaganda,"** has written; "The attack is emanating from both the media and politically, resulting in the rise we are seeing in attacks on Muslims, and the subsequent glossing over, normalization, and justification of such incidences. There is no dispute, however, about whether such fascism is on the rise-but there does seem to be an argument over whether or not the foul treatment of Muslims is just, and given that Islamophobia is clearly a distinct phenomenon and nothing seems to be working to counter this tide of racism.

From daily occurrences of racism picked up to by the mainstream, to an overt and covert policy seeking to divide and ruin Muslim lands and people, the advance towards fascism is undeniable, the trajectory remaining unchanged since 2001 and the birth of the New World Order. Of course, many groups are persecuted the world over, including within Europe and the US, but the rise in Islamophobia and attacks on Muslims, with everyday examples of casual racism witnessed almost daily, continues to be perpetuated from the top down as part of political policy.

But the problem goes beyond the realm of politics. It has become a cultural war, as well, with silly films, like *"American Sniper,"* proving to be about as helpful to Muslims and as accurate as the film *"Jaws"* was to sharks. The cultural narrative all too often masquerades as patriotism, while the people doing bad things rarely believe they are doing bad things. It's a battle on many fronts. Just like Islamic State has a savvy media campaign, so too do the Islamophobes, and often with the same paymasters.

In the US, the Islamophobia industry is thriving, with the likes of Pamela Geller spearheading various malicious campaigns, including anti-Muslim posters on subway trains depicting Muslims as criminals and barbarians. For a nation that took part, and is taking part, in the genocide of Muslim peoples in their own lands, and at the same time embrace as normal and acceptable such blatant racism, truly beggars belief.

People often argue that the vast majority of citizens do not conform to this form of racism. But then if such racism persists what difference does it make to those on the receiving end if those who claim to not be racist or Islamophobic remain silent? If a judge rules that racist posters depicting Muslims as savages are acceptable, but racism elsewhere is decried, then surely we rob the word racism of all meaning."........

Why so much intolerance, hatred and violence? Xenophobia and bigotry has been weaponized, atmosphere is thick with hatred, religious wars and violence, dangerous sign for the entire humanity.

People around the World become victim of propaganda, it is because most of the people are **NOT** Intellectually Competent.

Because people are not intelligent that is why they commit blunder and are susceptible, inspired by all the wrong things in life, weak minded people have absolutely no confidence in themselves hence they seriously believe or are forced to believe in divine intervention and allege God to perform miracles to solve their problems. Have a perspective, challenge your perspective will help you make right choices and take correct decisions.

In 2nd and 3rd century AD, when Christianity was formed for strategic reason by "Roman emperor **Constantine**," Christian terrorism had destroyed millenniums old ancient Pagan European culture and civilization, all pre-historic records were stolen and hidden or destroyed completely, fabulous ancient European history was decimated and rewritten, great archaeological sites and structures, artistic work, artefacts, paintings and scriptures were all burnt or hidden. When Islam came into effect in 7th century AD, the Islamists terrorists destroyed much of Paganism in Persia and central Asia, Islam's **jihadi army** ransacked villages and townships of Pagans and destroyed prehistoric primitive era art and culture. Christianity destroyed Paganism in Europe and in 21st century the Islamic army in disguise has entered Europe with clear objective to conquer Europe and America and establish Islamic Sharia rule.

Worldwide nearly 77% of educational institutes "schools, colleges and universities" are finance and funded and fully controlled by Christian missionaries trust and churches or by the Islamists organizations and governments, therefore prehistoric history is doctored and presented in such a way that suits their religious purpose, children for generations have been thought wrongs things, misleading information misguides youngsters, believes wrong things which makes them more superstitious, insular belief, because people in schools and universities learn incorrect facts of human history and various religions hence the in real life they behave abnormally therefore so much chaos and tension in society.

Islam and Christianity to large extent are responsible for hunger, poverty and homelessness in the world.

Islam and Christianity are copycat plagiarized version of paganism, all major Christian and Islamic festivals are not of their own but millennium old ancient pagan festivals, be it "Christmas and Easter" were celebrated and ritual were performed accordingly much before Christianity came into effect in Arabian region as well in roman Europe, Christian symbol **Cross** is/was also a pagan symbol, similarly Islam festivals Ramadan fasting was observed by various pagan religions and use to celebrate Eid-al-Fitr, also the so-called Islam's holiest site **Kaaba** in Mecca present day in Saudi Arabia, Kaaba was a medieval era Pagan temple and the annual Hajj that Muslims performs at Kaaba is or was actually a pagan ritual, also according to some findings Islamic God "**Allah**" is none other than the pagan god "**lord Shiva**," both Islam and Christianity have spread false belief and have severely misguided the large world's population, from childhood itself followers of Islam and Christianity are coerce and brainwashed to such an extent that they in their life time never really are ready to change their thoughts and thinking and blindly continue thinking in power of alleged **God**.

There is nothing divine, unique or exclusive in Christianity and Islam, with regards to Islam and Christianity, I have this say "**Old Wine filled in even Older Bottle > than, re-labelled >re-branded > repackaged and then through extensive sales promotion and marketing sold to the consumers and frivolous consumers without going into details or verifying authenticity, started buying and consuming wine**." People buy medicines and other food items without checking expiry dates and other vital information regarding the product, sexy girls and handsome men models services used for brand promotion to entice people to buy products. Similarly people starts believing in religion and cult or trust fortune tellers and astrologers, fools follow the foolish without applying their own mind and do not bother to establish the truth.

Who created whom? Humans created God a figment of our imagination or god created human beings.

People throughout history have created a god to meet their own needs and circumstances. But, the REAL God of the Universe cannot be the creation of mere man's logic and mental comprehension.

We are not "God," but our desire to be such takes us to madness.

It is extremely important for us homo-sapiens to be inspired and encouraged by all the right things in life, we need to spend time with person/persons who are more experienced, knowledgeable and intelligent than us so that we benefit from their know-how and knowledge all these will help us in our development and progress. But do a reality check and you'll find exactly the opposite. Great people large population in our world is/are inspired by all the wrong things in life, people waste their time and money on unnecessary unproductive things people purchase stuff which they don't use, people make friends with such type of people who are bigger duffer and inexperienced than them, not many prefer to watch or listen scholarly debates and discussions, mindless people are disinterested in intellectual minds discussing and debating critically important world-matters, people feel it is boring and time wasting reading inspirational and motivational scientific and philosophical books or articles in newspapers. Say it influence of evil spirit if you like, but overwhelming majority of people in our world likes to spend time and money on movie actors and sports personalities, watching movies and sports or talk-shows and fashion shows, people with great interest read inconsequential petty biographies and autobiographies of movie actors and fashion models as well of sports players.

Movies and TV serials promotes nothing but Sex, vulgarity and profanity, violence and gibberish uninspiring drama. With regards to sports most of the leading sports there is maximum corruption, people watch sports games and matches which apparently are alleged to have been fixed. So, majority of people do not like listening to scientists and philosophers, but, finds it more interesting and worthwhile watching movies and movie actors, they like to read personal information and other gossips of movie actors and fashion models. Great people are less concern about their own health and finances but are more bothered about movie actors and fashion models personal life. Movies be it Hollywood (American movies) or Bollywood (Hindi movies) promotes sex and violence, drug addiction and alcoholism is glorified, spread of vices and performance of evil and corrupt, music videos effectively glamourizes wild habits and promoting underage drinking and smoking.

Remaining time in life people like to waste practicing religion, unprecedented time in life is wasted performing religious ritual and in seeking divine blessing. Parents indoctrinates mind of their children from early childhood instilling fear in minds of their children that it is **God** in whom they should trust, god is their sole protector and saviour, and if they do not abide by rules of god there will be consequences if this allege god gets angry he/she (**God'** rather bizarre these devout religious people do not know the true gender of god) will punish you and you'll than have to regret all your life, so, this is how generation after generation children minds are brainwashed and instead of loving humans and serving cause of humanity they are more focussed on serving their respective religion's purpose, therefore this is precise reason for colossal violence and hate crimes around the world.

Are we to believe that there exists <u>Good spirit</u> and <u>Bad spirit</u>, bad spirit > we also call it **evil spirit**, good spirit guides us to safety and prosperity and evil spirit inspires us to adopt corrupt and unprincipled means of life to harm others as well to harm and destroy our own-self, just twisting the sentence to describe it is **"ascendancy of evil over good."** The Devil misleads people through spirit mediums, fortune-tellers, and those who practice divination or astrology. Drug use, hypnotism, and meditation techniques that empty the mind also expose a person to demon control. There are some malicious spirits that actively want to destroy the happiness of the people in this world. Astrology is science and NOT magic.

It is always so difficult "what to believe and what not to believe," – "who to trust and who not to trust," *"it is the choice we make and decisions we take"* that will have far reaching consequences, but one thing I would say with conviction that **"99% of world's population is intellectually incompetent,"** intellectual bankruptcy is prevalent. So as to defeat the evil and prevent evil from taking full control of your mind it is important for you to be on a positive **wavelength**, improve your thinking skills have a positive approach towards life, have a strong body language, evil can only gain control of a person who is feeble and gullible, so you become more intelligent and self-confident no evil will ever dare to come closer to you.

How to solve the problems that Islamic extremism and terrorism has created? How to end brutal religious wars and sectarian conflicts without firing a single bullet and without -- no one being killed? Can religious extremism and terrorism be defeated without any combative missions without any army's intervention? Yes indeed, Islam can't be or you'll never be able to defeat Islam by use of force, army sent into Islamic countries bombing villages and townships killing people, all such actions will fail as it has until now it is evidence the more armed force attacks the Islamists the more strong Sunni-Islam emerges, kill few thousand Sunni terrorists and many more thousands of Sunni are ready to fight, so your bullets will get over but the flow of Sunnis entering jihad (holy war) will not come to an end, therefore, there is more humble way and non-violent way to defeat Sunni-Islam extremism and terrorism and to Defeat Sunni-Islam once and for all,

World's largest <u>petroleum oil producer and exporter</u> "**Saudi Arabia**" apparently is world's biggest importer of arms and ammunition and defence equipment, Saudi imports Tens of Billions of dollar worth of arms and fighter jets aircrafts, principally sources most of arms and fighter aircrafts from America and Britain, Saudi Arabia as well got involved in Islamic religious wars that started post <u>Arab Spring revolution in 2011</u>, religious wars and sectarian conflicts in Islamic countries mainly being fought between two of Islam denomination <u>Shiite</u> and <u>Sunni</u>, Saudi being a prominent wealthy Sunni nation is/was in direct conflict with its impoverished neighbour **Yemen**, exclusively and specifically targeting and harming the **Houthi Shia** population inside Yemen, the Sunni dominated Saudi army blasting bombs and firing missiles at "Schools, hospitals and residential localities," in Yemen, Saudi army committed barbaric genocide, between 2015 and 2016 more than Ten thousand Shias mostly women and children were killed by Saudi army. Yemen is the most poorest country in the world, due to escalating tension between Sunnis and Shias, and chronic sectarian conflict millions of Yemenis have no access to water and medicines besides there are millions of people who homeless and have no source of income, Saudi Arabia and its allies other Sunni Arab countries ostentatiously are/were using the arms and weapons that they have purchased from the western countries. American, German, French and British governments did nothing and made no sincere effort to stop the war they maintained stoic silence, while Saudi and its Sunni allies are attacking the Shia population in Yemen.

Unabated Islamic religious wars and sectarian conflicts in Islamic world is an opportunity for the defence equipment and military hardware manufacturers to sell their sophisticated weapons and other communication and explosive devices to both the mainstream military as well the various terrorist groups who all are their valued customers, the middlemen and arms dealers are profiting immensely. *War for profit*, be it in America or south-America or in Islamic countries, Gun violence, crimes, terrorism and conflicts opens up huge opportunity for arms dealers and manufacturers of weapons to sell weapons to warring factions and profit from it. That is what it has proved to be true, the much talked about **war on terror** which was started by the then American President **Mr George W Bush** in 2001 with the purpose to eradicate and destroy Islamic terrorism has achieved nothing significant or meaningful in fact have only made bad situation even more worse, the world has become even more unsafe, accept the rich and the <u>Wall street Nabobs</u>, and large Multinational corporates have significantly benefitted from wars and conflicts, but as far as the common people is concern it is an unending ordeal. Between 2002 and

2015 U.S.A. alone have spent an estimated amount of $2 Trillion however some estimates also suggest more than U.S$4 trillion is spent on fighting War on Terror which also includes cost incurred fighting 2 wars one in Afghanistan and other in Iraq.

Terrorism, like war, is a hellish cliché of spin bloat, except for those who grab the gold, and who laugh at believers of endless threats ever-aborning in intelligence analysts' terrifying sadism: if you doubt us, ponder this historical blunder. As if more WTCs, and worse, rogue-heaved WMDs, are to be expected, now that underpinnings of MAD are an inside, classified, joke. Celebrity and fame should be its own reward, no need to lay on redundant wealth as well. Admirers of stars will underwrite their addiction to narcissism. Wealth accumulated and protected by dangerous hard labour -- by low-rank service members, cops and spooks, and their compatriots in industry -- should be distributed to those who face torture, mutilation and death for criminally-low wages -- and whose death families are assaulted by pre-positioned bugles, medals, flags and condolences.

Between 2001 till 2016 as a result of <u>War on terror</u> and <u>Islamic religious wars</u> an estimated 2 million people have been killed or have died unnatural death due to terrorism related violence and social chaos due to hunger and poverty in mostly Islamic and Muslim dominated countries in west-Asia and other Muslim dominated Asian and African countries. Worst affected and brutally harmed are countries such as "Syria, Yemen, Somalia, Afghanistan, Pakistan and of course Iraq from where it all began first in 1991. Few other Islamic countries such as "Turkey, Libya and Egypt" are/were other major trouble spot, Libya almost a failed state total anarchy complete breakdown of economic and political system, while Egypt and Turkey experienced increase in terror activities and massive rise in killings.

Islamists arrogance is responsible for so much bloodbath all over the world, who has failed whom' did the people followers of Islam failed their religion (Islam)? Or, has the religion (Islam) have failed its followers (people who follow Islam)? It is the latter, their religion "Islam" that has failed its followers, because the **documented constitution** of Islam and its core value is violent and preaches hatred instead of uniting it teaches to practice division, Islamists firmly believes that Islam is the best and supreme religion than compare to every other religion and their determined belief that Islamists are privilege people hence being born a Muslim makes them superior in every aspect and that followers of all other religions and or unbelievers are ugly creation of god so they are inferior and that non-Muslims are not worth calling humans worse than dogs and cats hence are **infidels** and infidels are equal to evil therefore harming or even going as far as to killing the infidels is considered as holy duty of each Muslim and that's why these ill-conceived jihadists (holy warrior) are so resolutely out in open to eliminate all the non-Sunni Muslim population across the world. But is the approach and is it the right strategy to counter Islamic extremism and stop the menace of Jihadists killings of non-Muslims therefore in retaliation attack the Jihadists in their strong hold in Islamic countries where they are hiding and operating from.

American, Russian, French and also British army targeting the Jihadists or to say Islamic terrorists camps in Islamic countries resorting to blasting bombs, aerial bombardments, indiscriminate firing missiles and bullets on pretext of eliminating the terrorists, since these jihadists and terrorists hide and are provided shelter in towns and cities and blended among civilian population therefore frequent attacks by American and Russian army results in deaths of many more people most of whom are civilians. Fighting "fire with fire," tit for tat strategy is false and flawed strategy highly unyielding and will never ever succeed in subduing the **Islamic jihadi project**, in fact the more the western and Russian army attacks Muslim dominated areas and more killing only helps the jihadists cause as it encourages more Muslim youths to fight **jihad** (Islam' religious holy war) against the enemy (from Muslims perspective all those people in this world who do not pledge their allegiance to their prophet Muhammad and do not believe in Allah are considered as enemy of Islam). This is precise reason as to why *War on terror* has failed and instead Islam has become more stronger because the more the killings of Muslims it polarizes the society and divides world's population, so even more non-Muslim leftist leaning people come out in open and supports Islam.

Human lives matter, no matter what religion you follow or do not follow any religion, regardless of your ethnicity or skin colour, killing of people is never justifiable, be it a member of mainstream official army or a terrorist, we all after all are humans, whether it is Muslim jihadis who kills non-Muslims or the non-Muslim security forces in retaliation kills jihadists or by default other unarmed Muslims, no matter who dies it has to be construed as crime against humanity, we are all humans, human lives matter, therefore in retaliation to jihadists terror attacks > attacking Muslim dominated areas is not a good strategy, but than if a large section of world's population is flawed and behaving like an **evil** who wants to destroy humanity we can't keep silence and do nothing, <u>here is a solution</u> "similarly like economic and trade and diplomatic sanctions are impose on a country that flouts international rules creates problems for other countries and whose government is brutal dictatorial and harms and supresses their people and also pose threat to other countries around the world, like for example all kinds of punitive economic and diplomatic sanctions are impose on North-Korea for its allege role in harming world's peace, stringent sanctions were impose on Iran for its allege Nuclear programme and so many more countries including Russia have experienced sanctions in history and also in present times," similarly to subjugate and to neutralize the power of Islam and to thrash its arrogance for that the non-Sunni Muslim population the powerful American, Russian and European countries should **impose strict economic and diplomatic sanctions on Islam and on Islamists**, social boycott of Muslims till such time they disband their barbaric religious Islamic doctrine and stop treating other non-Muslims like 2nd grade inferior citizens, this is the only way to defeat the Islamists, a most honourable and effective strategy which will be absolutely eco-friendly, no violence and no killings, what more it will be absolutely cost free no money will be spent and problem is sorted out *once and for all*, Islamists will never ever dare to challenge the non-Muslim population of the world and will be force to respect humanity will learn to respect people of every other religion and the unbelievers.

If there are problems there are solutions but who is ready and willing to work to solve most pressing human problems, people in this world are inspired by all the wrong things that's why with false impression and faulty ideas in their mind they practice all the wrong things which works against humanity and have deadly consequences. Don't wait for others to take the first step, have a positive and determined approach towards life, you be the first to do things and show it to the world --- yes' it works, yes it makes the difference and brings about change for the betterment.

In the catastrophic or accidental view of history we are led to believe that historical events, such as wars and revolutions were the direct result of some sudden or surprising event. While the catastrophic view is accurate for weather, volcanoes and earthquakes, it does not always provide a realistic view of humanity and events influenced by man. We believe that current world events are not simply circumstantial, but the result of an organized campaign by an elite group of unseen and widely unknown world leaders. Their goal is to exercise absolute dictatorial control over the world, to establish a **New World Order.**

It is better to walk alone rather than walk with the crowd who are all walking in the wrong direction.